Cambridge

Elements in Race, Ethnicity, and Politics
edited by
Megan Ming Francis
University of Washington

WALLS, CAGES, AND FAMILY SEPARATION

Race and Immigration Policy in the Trump Era

Sophia Jordán Wallace
University of Washington

Chris Zepeda-Millán
University of California–Los Angeles

CAMBRIDGE
UNIVERSITY PRESS

CAMBRIDGE
UNIVERSITY PRESS

University Printing House, Cambridge CB2 8BS, United Kingdom

One Liberty Plaza, 20th Floor, New York, NY 10006, USA

477 Williamstown Road, Port Melbourne, VIC 3207, Australia

314–321, 3rd Floor, Plot 3, Splendor Forum, Jasola District Centre,
New Delhi – 110025, India

79 Anson Road, #06–04/06, Singapore 079906

Cambridge University Press is part of the University of Cambridge.

It furthers the University's mission by disseminating knowledge in the pursuit of
education, learning, and research at the highest international levels of excellence.

www.cambridge.org
Information on this title: www.cambridge.org/9781108795333
DOI: 10.1017/9781108894920

First published 2020

A catalogue record for this publication is available from the British Library.

ISBN 978-1-108-79533-3 Paperback
ISSN 2633-0423 (online)
ISSN 2633-0415 (print)

Additional resources for this publication at http://www.cambridge.org
/9781108795333

Cambridge University Press has no responsibility for the persistence or accuracy of
URLs for external or third-party internet websites referred to in this publication
and does not guarantee that any content on such websites is, or will remain,
accurate or appropriate.

Walls, Cages, and Family Separation

Race and Immigration Policy in the Trump Era

Elements in Race, Ethnicity, and Politics

DOI: 10.1017/9781108894920
First published online: September 2020

Sophia Jordán Wallace
University of Washington

Chris Zepeda-Millán
University of California–Los Angeles

Author for correspondence: Sophia Jordán Wallace, sophiajw@uw.edu;
Chris Zepeda-Millán, czm@ucla.edu

Abstract: US immigration policy has deeply racist roots. From his rhetoric to his policies, President Donald Trump has continued this tradition, most notoriously through his border wall, migrant family separation, and child detention measures. But who exactly supports these practices and what factors drive their opinions? Our research reveals that racial attitudes are fundamental to understanding who backs the president's most punitive immigration policies. We find that whites who feel culturally threatened by Latinos, who harbor racially resentful sentiments, and who fear a future in which the United States will be a majority–minority country, are among the most likely to support Trump's actions on immigration. We argue that while the President's policies are unpopular with the majority of Americans, Trump has grounded his political agenda and 2020 reelection bid on his ability to politically mobilize the most racially conservative segment of whites who back his draconian immigration enforcement measures.

Keywords: Trump, border wall, immigration, family separation, child detention

ISBNs: 9781108795333 (PB), 9781108894920 (OC)
ISSNs: 2633-0423 (online), 2633-0415 (print)

Contents

A further Online Appendix can be accessed at
http://cambridge.org/9781108795333

1 Introduction

> When Mexico sends its people . . . They're bringing drugs. They're bringing crime. They're rapists . . .
>
> – Donald Trump, 2015

From the Constitution's only mention of migration – a reference guaranteeing the continuation of slavery – to our first Congress' decision to limit American citizenship to "free white persons," US immigration legislation has deeply racist roots (Ngai 2004; Johnson 2004; Molina 2014; Garcia Hernandez, 2019: 21). In line with this tradition, and, never one to be outdone, Donald Trump has undoubtedly become, in both his rhetoric and his enacted policies, the most blatantly anti-Latino and anti-immigrant president in modern American history. Over the four years of his first term, he has not only demonized, made racist comments about, and justified violence against Mexican and Central American immigrants, but has also allowed white nationalists like Stephen Miller and Steve Bannon to shape his immigration policies. The president has tried to end temporary protected status for hundreds of thousands of vulnerable Latin American, Caribbean, and African migrants; capped the number of refugees allowed into the United States at historic lows; made it harder to qualify and file for asylum; and violated international laws by forcing asylum seekers to "wait" in dangerous Mexican border towns. Trump has also attempted to ban Muslim immigrants from entering the country, deported undocumented youth activists (i.e., "Dreamers"), tried to end the Deferred Action for Childhood Arrivals program, expanded the number of immigrants subject to expedited removal, and created a new section of the Department of Justice dedicated to denaturalizing immigrants. His administration has also substantially increased local–federal immigration law enforcement agreements (i.e., 287(g)), further restricted prosecutorial discretion in cases involving undocumented immigrants, and boosted the number of US Immigration and Customs Enforcement (ICE) arrests by 40 percent, among other nativist actions (Moreno 2016; Garcia Hernandez, 2019: 6; Hayden 2019; Hing, 2019: 297–299; Wadhia, 2019: vii; Department of Justice 2020).

Given the array of anti-immigrant policies promoted by this administration and the devastating effects they have had on millions of people, why limit this Element to walls, cages, and family separation? As we explain in Section 1.1, these three immigration enforcement practices are not only politically salient issues with severe material consequences and symbolic meanings, but they also help expose and remind us of the close links between racism and US immigration policies. Consequently, we felt it important to explore who supports these draconian measures, what factors drive their beliefs, and whether their opinions are amenable to change in response to information about the catastrophic consequences of these policies.

1.1 Race, Walls, and Cages

During Donald Trump's 2016 campaign rallies, by far the most popular slogan chanted by thousands of attendees was, "Build the wall! Build the wall!" Indeed, his promise to build a barrier along the US–Mexico boundary was the centerpiece of the political agenda that won Trump the White House. Since becoming president, he has attempted to deliver on his commitment by announcing an executive order, declaring a national emergency, issuing his first veto, deploying the National Guard, and initiating the longest government shutdown in American history – all in an attempt to build support for and construct his "great, great wall" along the United States' nearly 2,000-mile southern border. From the start of his presidential campaign, Trump has maintained that such a mammoth bulwark is needed in order to keep out Latino immigrants who he falsely claims are "rapists" who bring "crime" and "drugs" into the country (Mark 2018).

Irrespective of this type of blatantly bigoted discourse, many social scientists often underemphasize or fail to consider the role that racism plays in fueling American calls for border walls.[1] According to geographer Reece Jones (2017), the election of Donald Trump has "reemphasized the significant role of race in the expansion of border security and in society's ambivalence to the appalling violence borders do to the bodies of others" (viii). Jones contends that the "exclusionary policies that make borders so violent today are implemented in the name of the citizens of America ... by which their proponents really mean 'white Americans'" (viii). Given the United States' history of border expansion through indigenous colonization and genocide in the name of a white "Manifest Destiny," we find Jones's argument justifiable. Nonetheless, little to no survey evidence exists that explores the contemporary relationship between race and backing the idea of a border wall. Thus, we aim to help fill this lacuna by putting white racial attitudes and opinions about Trump's fortification proposal front and center in our analysis.

Race has also historically played a key role in the development of US immigrant detention policies. Today, for example, Ellis Island is widely known as one of the most iconic symbols of American "freedom and democracy." Yet, tellingly, it was built in the late 1800s during the influx of "non-white" Southern and Eastern European immigrants, and it served as the country's first federal detention center (Silverman, 2010: 4). More surprising to

---

[1] See Jonson 2009, Nevins 2010, and Lytle Hernandez 2010 for exceptions.

readers may be that by the mid-1950s, when Ellis Island permanently closed its doors, the United States had all but abolished its immigration detention policies. In what was described by the Republican Eisenhower administration as a step toward a more "humane administration of immigration laws," even the Supreme Court praised the ending of detention as reflecting "the humane qualities of an enlightened civilization" (Garcia Hernandez, 2019: 47). The virtual abolition of immigrant detention policies occurred at a time when the Southern and Eastern European migrants initially targeted by them had, for the most part, "become" white (Jacobson 1998; Alba and Nee 2003; Roediger 2018). That whiteness may have played a part in the ending of US immigrant detention, however, might also provide some clues as to why the policy of immigrant detention resurfaced with a vengeance and is at the top of Trump's presidential agenda. As we will see, not only was immigrant detention revived to an unprecedented degree in response to Latin American and Caribbean migration, but race continues to play an important role in shaping public opinion on family and child detention policies today.

1.2 Main Findings and Argument

Our research reveals that the vast majority of survey respondents oppose the president's most punitive immigration policies. Across the political spectrum, people overwhelmingly support the releasing of migrant minors to family members or sponsors, and back a host of rights and accommodations for children in the custody of immigration officials. We find that most people, moreover, do not support the idea of a border wall or believe a wall would bring about the outcomes that President Trump has promised: namely, stopping undocumented immigration, drugs, and terrorists from entering the country. These opinions are deeply polarized by party affiliation, with Republicans much more likely than Democrats and independents to support Trump's policies, especially the border wall. Yet even the most fervent border fortification backers express doubt that a wall would achieve its stated purposes.

But if these policies are so unpopular with the public, and even those who support them believe they are ineffective, why does the president continue to make walls and immigrant detention the cornerstones of his political agenda and reelection bid? We argue that the answer to this question may lie in the symbolic meanings these practices convey, and in their ability to politically activate the small but racially conservative segment of Americans who support the president's most draconian immigration policies. Recall that in 2016, Trump lost the popular vote and only won the electoral college by a razor-thin margin. He did so to a large degree by mobilizing white voters who harbored high levels of racial resentment and anti-immigrant sentiments (Jacobson, 2017: 20; Sides et al., 2017: 40; Hooghe & Dassonneville, 2018: 531–532; Schaffner et al., 2018: 10). Similarly, our statistical analyses show that people who feel culturally threatened by Latinos, who are racially resentful, and who fear a future in which the United States will be a majority-minority country are the most likely to support the president's wall, family separation, and child caging policies. In short, we find that while not all whites in the United States support Trump's most brutal border and detention practices, those with the most negative racial attitudes tend to. As such, we believe that despite widespread opposition, the president's most controversial actions on immigration are less about reflecting the public's policy desires than they are about electorally rousing a racially extreme faction of the white public. In Section 1.3, we explain the methodological approach and data that brought us to these conclusions.

1.3 Public Opinion and Immigration Policy

A wealth of scholarship examines public opinion on immigration. One dominant model centers on labor market competition (Hainmueller & Hopkins 2014), whereby workers view immigrants as competitors and are less supportive of policies allowing more immigrants (Malhotra et al. 2013); some studies that engage with this approach, however, have found only a limited role for economic explanations (Hainmueller & Hiscox 2007). Another approach focuses on how higher education levels are associated with less restrictive immigration attitudes (Citrin et al. 1997). Hainmueller and Hiscox (2010) contend that highly educated individuals adopt cosmopolitan ideals that lead them to be more supportive of policies that increase immigration levels. On balance, more research has found support for the role of education in shaping immigration attitudes than for the influence of labor market competition, though the precise mechanism by which education influences attitudes toward immigration continues to be debated.

Immigration has also increasingly become a divisive issue in the United States, with Republicans and Democrats adopting enormously different positions in a highly polarized era (Layman & Carsey 2006). Republicans and conservatives express positions less supportive of immigration than do Democrats and liberals (Wong & Ramakrishnan 2010; Wong 2017; Wallace & Wallace 2020). Under certain conditions, however, Republicans can support pathways to citizenship (Wallace & Wallace 2020) or policies that can be described as expansionist (Tichenor 2002). Hainmueller and Hopkins (2014) note that more research is needed on the role of partisanship and ideology in explaining contemporary immigration attitudes.

Another strand of this literature focuses on racial factors, such as prejudice and demographic changes, in driving immigration attitudes. Individuals with higher levels of ethnocentrism or prejudice are more supportive of restrictive immigration policies (Kinder & Kam 2010; Valentino et al. 2013). People who have a strong conception of American identity, which includes whether people were born in the country and are Christian (Schildkraut 2005), or who define Americanism in exclusive terms (Wong 2010), are also more likely to support restrictive policies. Demographic change may also be a key factor, where proximity to larger immigrant populations can result in more restrictive and negative views toward immigration and immigrants (Hopkins 2010; Newman 2013; Abrajano & Hajnal 2015), though others find muted effects of demographic change and suggest anxiety may be the actual driver of anti-immigrant sentiment (Brader et al. 2008; Wallace 2014a).

What is missing from this scholarship is an explicit focus on how racial attitudes, various types of threat, and negative group sentiments are key explanatory factors in understanding immigration attitudes.[2] Our contributions to this literature are threefold. First, we provide a needed analysis of attitudes toward a host of immigration policies. Past work examines attitudes toward immigrants and policies on immigration levels or policy solutions for the undocumented population. Opinion studies that focus on specific immigration policies, such as immigrant detention or the border wall, are uncommon and needed.[3] Second, we center the role of racial attitudes – including racial resentment, views on discrimination, and perceptions of cultural and demographic threat – in driving public opinion. Finally, we demonstrate how polarized opinion toward immigration policies is split along partisan lines. Our data shows that while factors such as partisanship are important in parsing differences in opinion, racial attitudes are also critical to understanding attitudes on an issue that is highly racialized.

1.4 Empirical Approach

To analyze attitudes toward immigration, we conducted an original survey called the Immigration in the Trump Era Survey (ITES). Our survey was conducted online in August 2019 by the survey firm Prolifics. The median completion time was fifteen minutes. Our sample of 1,109 white respondents is representative of the national US white population. Our analysis focuses on white respondents for several reasons. First, the most variation in opinion on immigration is found among whites (Abrajano & Hajnal 2015). This can be

---

[2] One exception is Pérez (2010), who demonstrates that implicit racial attitudes shape attitudes toward immigration policies.

[3] A key exception is the DREAM Act (see Wallace & Wallace 2020).

partially explained by significant variation in political ideology and partisanship: roughly half of whites are Democrats and half Republicans, with similar proportions of liberals and conservatives (Noel 2014; Junn 2017). This variation is particularly important when immigration politics is polarized along party and ideological lines, among elites and in the general public (Haynes et al. 2016). This is not to say that other racial groups do not express meaningful differences on immigration, but rather that the greatest divergence is expressed among whites.[4] By focusing on white attitudes, we are able to examine what drives both support for and opposition to immigration policies. Finally, we focus on a single group in order to fully explore differences within this group rather than simply compare groups to one another.

The survey included questions about various immigration policies, respondent's racial and ethnic identification, the strength of their racial and ethnic identity, and their perceptions of linked fate. The survey also contained questions measuring the respondents' perceptions of economic, demographic, and cultural threat; anti-immigrant sentiments and stereotypes; levels of racial resentment; political ideology; and political partisanship.[5] Sections 2, 3, and 5 of this study draw heavily on the observational survey data to examine the state of support for and opposition to immigration policies.

Finally, we conducted three survey experiments to examine the conditions under which immigration attitudes might shift. This approach is particularly useful given the amount of misinformation and misperceptions that mire the immigration debate (Chavez 2008; Haynes et al. 2016). Through this research design, we are able to directly assess whether information about the negative consequences of Trump's immigration policies decreases support for them. Our results provide little evidence that information moves opinion, however. Our analyses aim to achieve three goals: (1) to provide an assessment of overall levels of public support for some of Trump's signature immigration policies; (2) to analyze the most important factors in explaining support for and opposition to these policies; and (3) to identify the conditions under which support for or opposition to these policies can be shifted.

1.5 Salience of Immigration

We focus on immigration because it is a centerpiece of the Trump presidency and because its salience has increased dramatically. Historically, immigration has been identified as either the top issue or among the top three issues for Latinos (Wallace 2014b). Scholars suggest immigration is a highly personal issue for

---

[4] See Carter (2019) for Black attitudes, Fraga et al. (2011) for Latino attitudes, and Masuoka and
Junn (2013) for Latino and Asian-American attitudes.

[5] ITES offers a wealth of information on contemporary attitudes on Trump's immigration policies.
A full list of survey questions is in Appendix A.

Latinos and that Latinos tend to support policies expanding immigrant rights (Wallace 2012; Sanchez et al. 2015). Other racial groups have traditionally not attached comparable levels of importance to immigration (Rouse 2013). In the last five years, however, a growing proportion of whites have begun to rank immigration as a top issue, with large segments ranking it as their number-one issue (Abrajano & Hajnal 2015; ANES 2016 and 2018). Our survey data reveals that 21 percent of white respondents now rank immigration as a top-three issue.

But what is driving this increased salience? In examining differences by political party, a more nuanced picture of salience emerges. Among white Republicans, 42 percent rank immigration as a top-three issue. This level may indicate increasing anxiety about immigration and cultural threat. The dominant public discourse frames immigrants and immigration in deeply negative and pejorative ways, and this rhetoric has likely resulted in a greater proportion of the white population seeing immigration as an important issue. Increased issue salience thus might not always reflect desire for immigration reform that expands immigrant rights, as is the case for Latinos: it may instead indicate anxiety and support for restrictive policies (Abrajano & Hajnal 2015).

Immigration's increased salience has meaningful implications. Candidates, especially Trump, will likely continue to keep immigration at the forefront of their political agendas. Elites will adopt positions and seek to implement policies they believe will be popular with voters to whom immigration is highly salient. We may also observe an increase in the frequency of more explicit and negative rhetoric about immigration, since this rhetoric increasingly resonates with portions of the public. In this political environment, it is critically important to understand public attitudes toward Trump's immigration policies and the factors that drive support for and opposition to them.

1.6 Plan of the Element

The Element proceeds with three main sections analyzing opinion data, followed by a conclusion discussing the implications of our results. Sections 2 and 3 have a similar structure, beginning with a brief policy history and discussion of the symbolisms conveyed by border walls and migrant detention. We contextualize these practices with recent examples of how they have affected immigrants. The goal of each of these sections is to describe and analyze how and why these policies have manifested, as well as the key factors that drive current public support for and opposition to them.

More specifically, Section 2 centers on Trump's proposal to build a wall along the US–Mexico border. We analyze general levels of support and opposition, as well as whether individuals believe a wall would be effective in stopping undocumented immigrants, illegal drugs, and terrorists from crossing the border. Section 3 concentrates on the detention of children in immigration facilities and family separation. Our data focus on support for and opposition to these policies, as well as public opinion about the rights and accommodations migrant children should have while in detention. Section 4 turns to our experimental data to examine the conditions under which support and opposition to the wall, child detention, and family separation might shift. We assess whether providing information about the negative consequences and harms of all three policies can reduce support for them. Section 5 considers the implications of our findings for contemporary immigration politics with an eye toward the 2020 election and beyond.

1.7 Note on Terminology

In this Element, we have made a number of choices regarding terminology. We primarily use the term "undocumented" rather than "illegal" immigrants. This choice reflects contemporary best practice in scholarship and media, given the problematic nature and harmful impacts surrounding constructions of illegality (Jones-Correa & de Graauw 2013; Menjivar & Kanstroom 2013). The exception to this terminological choice was in survey question wording where we wanted to maintain consistency with past polls, or where we felt the usage of undocumented could fundamentally alter how respondents answered.[6] With regard to immigration detention facilities, considerable debate exists among the media, activists, and elites about whether to use "centers," "facilities," "concentration camps," or "prisons" (Katz 2019; Stolberg 2019). We employ the word "facilities" because we view it as the most neutral available term, and the one least likely to affect how respondents with different political ideologies and partisan identification might respond. We contend that "facilities" invokes neither a potentially positive-sounding place, as does "center" (with its echoes of a community or youth center), nor does it have the negative connotations of "camps," which often conjure memories of the Holocaust or Japanese internment.

---

[6] See Appendix A for question wording.

2 The Wall

Tear down this wall!

– President Ronald Reagan, 1987

BUILD THE WALL!

– President Donald Trump, 2017

The bulwark referred to by President Reagan in the first epigraph is the iconic Berlin Wall, whose fall was celebrated around the world. The German fortification had come to symbolize economic stagnation and the suppression of freedom, democracy, and human rights. For good reason, as the Cold War came to an end, border walls were seen as shameful embodiments of the totalitarian countries that built them to keep people fleeing poverty and repression from crossing. Thus, the idea of any nation constructing a massive and costly national boundary barrier seemed anachronistic (Jones, 2012: 5). In fact, many observers at the time believed we had entered a new and interdependent era of capitalist globalization that would lead to "the rollback of the state and the erosion of its borders," including the walls that sometimes delineate them (Andreas, 2000b: 2; Ohmae 1999).

Although the international system has become more economically interconnected, contrary to expectations, the stigma associated with the erecting of walls has all but vanished, as "the current era of globalization has resulted in the most intensive and extensive period of bordering in the history of the world" (Jones & Johnson, 2016: 1). Importantly, and as the second epigraph illustrates, border walls are not solely an international phenomenon but are presently at the center of US politics. This raises a number of questions. How could a country whose leaders once advocated for the tearing down of walls elect a president who ran on a platform promising to build one? How can we explain the contemporary clamoring for an American border barrier, and what factors drive support for this proposal? Before exploring these vital questions, we examine what previous research tells us about what walls symbolize, why countries build them, and what they signify about the people who demand them. Additionally, we provide a brief review of some of the major policies – and their effectiveness – that over several decades have led to the construction of about 700-miles of fortifications along the 2,000-mile US–Mexico border.

2.1 Why Walls?

Prominent scholars agree that border bulwarks "have always spectacularized power" and aimed to evoke permanence, security, and impenetrability (Sorel, 2014: 136; Brown, 2017: 51). State border fortifications convey two messages: one of deterrence to the unsanctioned would-be crossers outside of them, and one of reassurance to the citizens living behind them (Nieto-Gomez, 2014: 193). Walls "reflect the nature of power relations and the ability of one group to determine" lines of separation (Newman, 2006: 147), often excluding "suspicious outsiders on ethnic, racial, and social grounds" (Golunov, 2014: 123). In the process, they attempt to preserve an imagined – often white – national homogeneity, distinguishing those who demographically belong from those who do not.

The people on "the other side" of walls are almost always seen as ungoverned and uncivilized, and are described in dehumanizing ways that make them seem unworthy of human rights or even of human life itself (Jones, 2012: 15: De Leon 2015). Hence, walls not only serve as markers of state sovereignty, they also symbolize the reaffirmation of identities. They are instruments of division and tools for the "othering" of foreignness (Newman & Paasi, 1998: 189; Vallet & David, 2014: 142). Viewed through this lens, the recent worldwide increase in xenophobia and populism has manifested itself in a racialized, nativist backlash embodied by the desire for border barriers (Longo, 2018: 2).

How can we best understand racist calls for walls in a globalized era that was supposed to be unifying and borderless? According to Longo (2018), since the September 11 attacks, immigration and terrorism "have dominated the global political imaginary" (2018: 1). Not surprisingly, then, the top reasons contemporary governments – including the United States – give to justify their construction of border bulwarks are their desires to stop undocumented migration (57 percent), terrorism (28 percent), and smuggling (24 percent) (Vallet, 2019: 158–159). Yet, as we will see, at least in the case of the United States, walls have not been effective in achieving their stated goals. So why erect them?

Rather than create a more unified and equitable world order, the post–Cold War era of global capitalism has exacerbated both domestic and international economic inequalities, often along racial lines (Harvey 2007; Jones 2012; Stiglitz 2018). These extreme financial disparities contribute to or directly create the supply of and demand for international migration, including clandestine migration (Sassen 1988; Sassen 2014). Tellingly, quantitative studies on border wall building have shown that the countries that construct them share one primary commonality: major differences in wealth between them and the neighbors they seek to block out (Hassner & Wittenberg 2015; Carter & Poast 2017). As Jones and Johnson (2016) put it, border barriers have essentially "become lines for the protection" of resources amassed by rich nations (9). According to Brown (2017), border walls help "organize deflection from crises of national cultural identity, from colonial domination in a postcolonial age, and from the discomfort of privilege obtained through superexploitation in an increasingly interconnected and interdependent global political economy" (145). As a result, the citizens of Western countries convince themselves that they are the true victims of globalization (133–134; Hochschild 2018), not the people of the global South who have disproportionately suffered from the effects of colonization and capitalist exploitation.

Although the carceral and defense industries have found the "business of bordering" (Fernades 2007; Andersson 2014) to be a lucrative one in which they spend millions on lobbying in return for billions in profits (see Section 3), the rise of global capitalism – or racial capitalism, to be more exact – has led to open borders for the members of mostly white Western nations, but border fortifications for the negatively racialized people of so-called Third World nations. Thus, national boundary walls serve the purpose of global wealth and resource hoarding, limiting the mobility of transnationally displaced labor, and in the process they help maintain vast socioeconomic divisions between wealthy and impoverished countries – "divisions that often correspond to conventional notions of race, in addition to ethnicity and nationality," and which can be described as a system of "global apartheid" (Sharma 2007; Nevins, 2010: 205; Loyd, Mitchelson, & Burridge 2012).

Before explaining how the latter insights help us understand America's current calls for walls, in the following section we present a short sketch of US border fortification legislation over the last several decades.

2.2 US Border Bulwark Policies

For most of the nineteenth and twentieth centuries, only a few hole-filled fences sporadically dotted the nation's southern boundary. While Richard Nixon was the first president to propose building a barrier along the entire US–Mexico border (Grandin 2019), it was President Carter who began materializing this plan by building sections of fencing along it (Dunn, 1996: 183). No additional fortifications were constructed under President Reagan; however, he was the first president to send National Guard troops to the border. Reagan framed illegal immigration as a national security issue, claiming that "tidal waves" of refugees, narcotics, and terrorists were infiltrating the United States from Mexico (Dunn, 1996: 42; Argueta, 2016: 13). In other words, while he was calling for the tearing down of concrete walls abroad, Reagan was also helping to create the rhetorical template that future presidents would use to build steel walls at home. When George H. W. Bush assumed the Oval Office in 1989, he continued to escalate the policing of the southern border. One of the most controversial aspects of these efforts was his 1991 construction of a seven-mile wall between San Diego and Tijuana, a move consistent with the 1990 Immigration Act that, among other provisions, called for the building of "structures to deter illegal entry" into the country (Nevins, 2010: 86). By the time Bush left office, about thirty miles of new or repaired fencing, most of it wall-like, marked the US–Mexico borderline (Dunn, 1996: 136).

Upon entering the White House, President Clinton followed his signing of the North American Free Trade Agreement (NAFTA) with what, up until then, was the largest degree of border militarization in US history, including more than doubling the miles of wall and various policing campaigns such as Operation Gatekeeper (Andreas 2000; Nevis 2010). Several key events of the early 1990s propelled this process: a terrorist bombed the World Trade Center, the "War on Drugs" was raging, and the national media highly sensationalized its coverage of undocumented Latino immigration (Andreas 2000; Santa Ana 2002). In this context, Clinton signed the Republican-sponsored Illegal Immigration Reform and Immigrant Responsibility Act (IIRIRA) in 1996. Among its many punitive provisions, IIRIRA was the first law to authorize the attorney general's office to construct border fencing, giving it the power to waive a pair of environmental laws to do so (Haddal et al., 2009: 4–5). Activists quickly raised several ecological concerns and legal challenges, holding up some of the planned wall building in court (Herweck & Nicol, 2018: 13). Nonetheless, by the time Clinton's tenure was over, one hundred miles of fortifications had been completed (Wong, 2017: 63), and the precedent of waiving laws to build walls was set.

Ironically, President George W. Bush built no border barriers immediately after the September 11 attacks. Less than two miles were constructed during his entire first term. Instead, from 2001 through 2003, Bush focused on starting wars in Afghanistan and Iraq and on creating what eventually became the Department of Homeland Security (DHS), which consumed and renamed the Immigration and Naturalization Service (INS) and other agencies. This was a critical transformation because it signified that national security and border security were no longer discrete domains (Longo, 2018: 3). Reagan's rhetorical framing of migrants, smugglers, and terrorists as security threats had become an institutional reality.

With the establishment of the DHS, "attention returned to the Mexican border as concerns about terrorist infiltration were overlaid with representations of Mexico as an ungoverned and uncivilized place" (Jones, 2012: 39, 41). During this period, Bush happily signed the 2005 REAL ID Act. Although the bill focused on creating federal standards for government identification cards, conservatives in Congress inserted an amendment that gave the DHS the unprecedented authority to waive "*all legal requirements*" to ensure expeditious construction of border fortifications (Haddal et al., 2009: 6; Herweck & Nicol, 2018: 17). Combined with these new legal powers, the following year's bipartisan 2006 Secure Fence Act (SFA) provided the financial and institutional support needed for the explosion of wall building that occurred during Bush's second term. According to Wong (2017), the SFA authorized the DHS to take "all actions" necessary to "control the border" and provided it with the resources to accomplish this goal (61). Between 2006 and 2007, the amount spent on border fencing and tactical infrastructure jumped astronomically, from $300 million to $1.5 billion, a 400 percent increase (62). SFA required "no less than 700 miles" of fencing along five segments of the US–Mexico border (Argueta, 2016: 14). Thus, the cumulative effects of Bush's actions were that border fencing went from fewer than 150 miles when he entered office to over 600 miles of fortifications by the time he exited (Wong, 2017: 64).

During a 2008 presidential campaign visit to the border, then-senator Barack Obama expressed regret for supporting the SFA. Obama told local leaders that he was "now opposed to the idea of the wall" and that if he were elected, "something would be done" about it (Garrett, 2009: 129). Yet, in some respects, Bush's unparalleled bulwark building continued after he left office, not because of what Obama did but because of what he permitted. During his first year as president, Obama allowed over 100 miles of border walls funded under his predecessor to go forward (Herweck & Nicol, 2018: 54). He also continued to increase funding for Border Patrol agents and other immigration enforcement measures like deportations. After Obama's initial year in the White House, however, funding for fencing was cut dramatically, and wall construction stagnated during the remainder of his presidency (Argueta, 2016: 15).

2.3 Do Walls Work?

In terms of effectiveness, the border was more militarized and had more fortifications on 9/11 than at any previous point in US history, yet the attacks still occurred. All the hijackers entered the country with visas through formal ports of entry and eventually flew airplanes into buildings – none of which would have been prevented by a border wall. Perhaps this is why, despite the burst of walls that emerged around the world after September 11 (Vallet, 2019: 156–157), studies have found that "there is no statistical relationship between actual levels of terrorism and the propensity of states to construct walls" (Hassner & Wittenberg, 2015: 174). Research also shows, moreover, that "despite widespread alarms raised," there is no evidence of terrorists entering the United States from – or of even the presence of terrorists in – Mexico (Leiken & Brookes, 2006: 503). In fact, since 9/11, domestic terrorists – the vast majority of whom are not immigrants but white, right-wing, US-born citizens – have killed more Americans than international terrorists have (Byman 2019).

With regard to drug smuggling, not only have over 220 underground tunnels from the Mexican to the US side of the border been discovered since the 1990s, but the massive increase in the volume of cross-border traffic caused by NAFTA has given cartels the ability to hide more of their narcotics shipments inside the increasing number of commercial and private vehicles entering the country (Nevins, 2010: 162). As a result, according to the US Drug Enforcement Administration, today the majority of illicit drugs continue to enter through official ports of entry (DEA 2018), not via the remote parts of the southwestern deserts where Trump wants to build his wall.

Although walls have not stopped the trafficking of narcotics, they do seem to have put more money in the coffers of drug cartels. The increased difficulty of entering the United States due to walling and militarization means that unauthorized migrants must now pay professional smugglers to help them cross the border. Not surprisingly, drug cartels control the most hidden routes and, as a result, have discovered a cash cow in the human smuggling business. As a former Border Patrol chief put it, "The more difficult the crossing, the better the business for the smugglers" (Andreas, 2000: 95–96). Tellingly, in the decade after NAFTA, which INS officials knew would *increase* undocumented migration (Nevins, 2010: 168), and since major border fortification began, the number of undocumented immigrants in the United States skyrocketed from 5.7 million in 1995 to 11.1 million in 2005 (Pew Research Center 2019). Statistical studies show that from the early 1990s to the present, the escalation in border fencing has failed to reduce clandestine migration (Wong, 2017: 168). In short, in terms of their stated goals, walls have failed to decrease or prevent terrorism, drugs, and undocumented immigration. Symbolically, however, their usefulness in contemporary racial politics is undeniable.

2.4 Trump's Walling

As of December 2019, after over three years in office, Trump had not managed to get a single mile of new border wall built (da Silva 2019). And while the president has repaired some parts of existing border bulwarks and claimed these updates are "impenetrable," Border Patrol officials admit that smugglers have already used a ladder to successfully climb over and an inexpensive saw to cut through the renovated parts of the wall (Miroff 2019). Nonetheless, the fact that the border wall is one of the cornerstone issues of Trump's political agenda and reelection bid suggests that whether or not he fulfills his promise to build over 400 miles of wall by the end of 2020 (Kumar 2020) is less significant than the wall's rhetorical usefulness in mobilizing his base and the symbolic meanings his pledge conveys.

Despite their material ineffectiveness, border fortifications can reassure panicked citizens that their government is working to protect them from always lurking, racialized foreign threats. In this fashion, Trump has discursively criminalized Latino immigrants, claiming they are "bad *hombres*" and "rapists" who bring "drugs" and "crime." The president has also dehumanized migrants by, describing them as "infesting" (Zimmer 2019) the country – a term usually reserved for pests and diseases – and disparagingly stating, "These aren't people. These are animals" (Korte & Gomez 2018). Because dehumanization and criminalization can be used to justify physical violence against demonized groups, it should not have surprised anyone when in 2019 a white man who had tweeted "#BuildTheWall" fatally shot twenty people (almost all of whom were Latino) in El Paso, Texas. Echoing Trump's language, he defended his mass murder as a "response to the Hispanic invasion" (Hasan 2019).

The usefulness of walls as instruments of division that aim to reaffirm certain – in this case, white – identities and preserve imagined (or desired) national homogeneity is also on full display in the rhetoric of the president himself. For example, he claimed it was "a shame" that immigration had "changed the fabric of Europe," and "not in a positive way," but in a manner that was leading to Europeans' "losing" their culture to migrants of color from the global South (Nguyen 2018). Trump doubled down on his white nationalism when he complained that the United States had too many immigrants from "shithole countries" (i.e., the regions of Latin America, the Caribbean, and Africa) while expressing his desire for more migration from Scandinavian nations (Kendi 2019). As our survey results show, the notion that migrants pose a cultural threat to the United States is key to understanding the support of some whites for the president's punitive immigration policies.

In sum, President Trump has used his calls for a border wall to foster racial fears and resentment, fanning the flames of white nationalism and demonizing migrants – especially Latino ones – by fueling bigoted conspiracy theories about the supposed cultural, political, and demographic dangers posed by them. In the process, he has attempted to reaffirm a need to preserve the United States as a white nation, demanded more white migration, and propagated false notions of white victimhood.

In the remainder of this section, we explore the degree to which these themes influence public support for Trump's proposal to build a mammoth wall along our southern border.

2.5 Public Opinion and Border Walls

Since the early 1990s, a number of studies have assessed public support for building a border wall. In 1993, Gallup found that 71 percent of respondents expressed opposition. By 1995, the percentage in opposition had decreased to 65 percent, and in 2006 was 56 percent. Since then, the level of opposition to a border wall has hovered in most Gallup polls between 56 and 60 percent (Norman 2019). Gravelle (2018: 108) found similar trends, showing opposition to the wall gradually increasing to 61 percent in 2016. For three decades, then, about half to a strong majority of the country has opposed building a wall. Given the salience of immigration and the frequency with which President Trump focuses on the imperative to build a wall, it is critical to assess the current state of public support. In this section, we seek to assess the factors driving contemporary support for and opposition to the wall, as well as public perceptions of its potential effectiveness.

Research focusing on how proximity to the border influences attitudes on immigration is fairly limited. Even fewer articles directly examine public support for a wall. Prior work has demonstrated that proximity to the US–Mexico border can substantially shape attitudes toward immigration policies, and this effect is largely polarized by political party. Proximity leads Democrats to be more supportive of initiatives protecting immigrants and to oppose restrictive policies, while it increases Republicans' willingness to support restrictive immigration policies and to oppose policies seeking to expand immigrant rights (Branton et al. 2007; Dunway et al. 2010; Gravelle 2016). But these studies do not focus on support for a border wall.

On the question of how proximity to the border influences opinions about the wall, the findings are mixed. Gravelle (2018) suggests that as distance from the border increases, both Democrats and Republicans, as well as liberals and conservatives, are less likely to support a wall. Cortina (2019), by contrast, asserts that people living in close proximity to the border learn and are socialized about the realities involved, and are consequently less likely to support constructing a border wall than those living farther away, who express opinions from a decontextualized point of view.

What is often missing from opinion studies on immigration is how racial attitudes, anti-immigrant sentiment, and perceptions of threat shape attitudes toward specific immigration policies such as the border wall. The role of these factors is particularly relevant given the highly racialized nature of the debate on the border wall, as well as the way in which it has become a symbol of anti-Latino and anti-immigrant sentiment. We therefore center the role of racial attitudes, anti-immigrant sentiments, and threat alongside partisanship in our analyses.

2.6 Methodological Approach

To examine contemporary attitudes toward Trump's proposal to build a wall, we designed survey items for the 2019 ITES specifically focused on support for the wall and perceptions of its effectiveness across several dimensions. For each component of public attitudes toward the wall examined, we first discuss the survey questions posed, then the overall levels of support for and opposition to those questions, before turning to statistical models to examine variation in the factors influencing opinions.

In all of our statistical models, we include a host of background control variables, including age, gender, income, and education. Age is measured as a categorical variable with six categories. Gender is coded where a value of 1 indicates the respondent is male and 0 female. Income is coded on a seven-point scale, as is education. To control for media consumption and the dominance of immigration coverage on Fox News (Radtke 2017), we also included a measure of whether people regularly watch Fox News. While income and education are variables frequently treated as controls, in the immigration attitudes literature they can be critical factors for explaining variation. Prior work demonstrates, for example, that higher education can lead to more progressive attitudes on immigration (Hainmueller & Hiscox 2010). Additionally, if individuals are motivated by economic concerns, some scholarship has shown that lower-income individuals are less supportive of pro-immigration policies (Hanson et al., 2009). The inclusion of these measures allows us to test whether the findings from these studies hold up when studying attitudes toward the border wall and other immigration policies.

Our primary explanatory variables in this Element are racial attitudes and partisanship, as well as cultural and demographic threat. Prior research has analyzed whether demographics drive anti-immigrant attitudes (Hopkins 2010; Newman 2013; Abrajano & Hajnal 2015), though often with mixed results. We theorize that what primarily drives any potential relationship between demographics and anti-immigrant attitudes is not actual demographics, but rather anxiety around demographic change. Our demographic threat measure asks, "The Census Bureau estimates that by 2045 racial minorities will compose the majority of the United States population. How concerned are you about this demographic change?" Because prior work has theorized that much of the backlash on immigration is rooted in the perceived threat of Latinos (US and foreign-born) (Chavez 2008; Abrajano & Hajnal 2015), we also include a Latino-specific measure of cultural threat. This question asks, "How concerned are you that immigration from Latin America is changing American culture?" Answer choices for both questions were "Not at All Concerned," "Slightly Concerned," "Somewhat Concerned," "Very Concerned," and "Extremely Concerned." The analytical advantage of these two measures of demographic and cultural threat is that they directly tap into perceptions of threat rather than making inferences from contextual factors.[7]

---

[7] See Appendix B for more discussion.

The primary variable used in opinion studies to examine racial attitudes is racial resentment. The racial resentment scale is created using four items that ask respondents to agree or disagree with the following statements: (1) Blacks should work their way up without any special favors; (2) Generations of slavery and discrimination make it difficult for Blacks to work their way out of the lower class; (3) Blacks have gotten less than they deserve; and (4) Blacks must try harder to get ahead. Answer choices range from "Strongly Disagree" to "Strongly Agree". The items are recoded to be in the same direction and placed on a scale from 0 to 1, with higher values indicating higher levels of resentment. While this scale was constructed to measure racial attitudes toward African-Americans (Kinder & Sanders 1996; Tuch & Hughes 2011), no similar scale was created or designed to measure racial resentment toward Latinos until 2020 (Ramirez and Peterson 2020). Scholars have utilized the racial resentment measure and found that high levels of racial resentment are associated with more restrictive and negative immigration viewpoints (Hajnal and Rivera 2014; Tesler 2016). In the absence of a Latino- or immigrant-specific measure at the time of our survey in 2019, we employed this standard measure of racial resentment in our analysis.

Another type of racial attitude that can influence policy opinions concerns perceptions of discrimination (Valentino & Brader 2011). We asked respondents to rate how much discrimination a racial or ethnic group faces on a scale from ranging from "none at all" to "a great deal." The most obvious group to inquire about, given the focus of this study, is immigrants. The racialization of immigration often results in stereotyping all Latinos as immigrants and all immigrants as Latino (Chavez 2008; Masuoka & Junn 2013; Zepeda-Millan 2014). Thus, we asked respondents how much discrimination they think Latinos and immigrants face. We think both of these survey questions are measures of progressive racial attitudes because respondents who answer "a lot" or "a great deal" recognize the substantial levels of discrimination faced by Latinos and immigrants today.

Recent work on racial attitudes also reveals that some segments of the white population increasingly worry about and believe whites experience discrimination (Jardina 2019). Consequently, to assess the degree to which they feel marginalized, we also ask respondents how much discrimination they felt whites face. We found it theoretically interesting and important to measure this phenomenon given that a disproportionate amount of power and wealth in the United States is held by white elites (King & Smith 2005; Masuoka & Junn 2013). Strength of white identity has also been recently shown to strongly influence racial attitudes (Jardina 2019). Accordingly, we ask respondents how important being white is to their identity. Finally, to assess whether respondents acknowledge the advantages bestowed on white people because of their skin color, we ask respondents if they agree or disagree with the following statement: "White people in the US have certain advantages because of the color of their skin." This is a measure of "white privilege," because those who agree with this statement are actively acknowledging the racial advantages of whites relative to other groups (Lopez-Bunyasi 2015).

To measure the impact of partisanship, we constructed a binary variable for Republican, where 1 represents a Republican and 0 represents a non-Republican. Additionally, in alternate models, we test the role of ideology using a seven-point scale, where lower values represent more liberal ideological scores and higher values are more conservative. In graphical and textual depictions of the survey results throughout the Element, we also show differences between Republicans, independents, and Democrats, as well as liberals, moderates, and conservatives.

The outcomes we are trying to explain in this section – levels of support for the wall and perceptions of the wall's effectiveness – have four answer choices ranging from "Strongly Disagree" to "Strongly Agree" or "Strongly Oppose" to "Strongly Support." We normalized the dependent variables to range between 0 and 1, and we use ordinary least squares (OLS) to estimate our statistical models. Explanatory variables have also been normalized for ease of interpretation of the results.[8]

2.7 Theoretical Expectations

We expect that party, ideology, cultural and demographic threat, and racial attitudes will drive support for the wall. Given the salient role of political party and ideology in examining immigration attitudes (Haynes et al. 2016; Wong 2017; Wallace & Wallace 2020), we expect Republicans and conservatives will be substantially more likely than Democrats and liberals to support building a wall. We expect there to be a strong relationship between party and wall support for several reasons. Most obviously, the policy is one of President Trump's signature issues. Second, the wall is widely supported by conservative and Republican political elites (Levine & Arkin 2019). Finally, the policy is a restrictionist immigration policy that is focused on enforcement, an increasingly dominant component in the Republican Party platform (Wallace 2014a; Wong 2017). Taken together, these considerations provide strong support for the theoretical expectation that wall support will be driven by party.

Because of the durable role of racial attitudes and threat in influencing public opinion on racialized policies (Kuklinski et al. 1997; Gilens 1999; Krysan

---

[8] Coding details of these variables are in Appendix A. The results do not significantly differ when estimating the models using ordered logit.

2000), including immigration (Peréz 2015; Casellas & Wallace 2019), and the symbolic purpose of the wall as an Othering device, we also expect these factors to be critical in explaining support for the wall. We expect that individuals with the highest levels of racial resentment will be considerably more likely to support the wall. Similarly, we expect people who express strong levels of cultural threat to be more likely to support the wall because they feel that immigrants from Latin America pose a threat to the United States (Chavez 2008). For these individuals, the wall may serve as both a symbol and as an example of good public policy. Similarly, those who are most worried about demographic changes in the population will be much more likely to support the wall for reasons similar to those driving people who are culturally threatened. When people feel threatened by demographic changes and perceive potential negative cultural changes from immigration, we theorize that they may be experiencing an existential crisis not only in their own identity, but also in their sense of national identity. In this way, they may perceive immigration and changing demographics as disrupting their place in society and what they understand American culture to be, triggering support for the border wall out of this sense of threat.

Turning to factors that reduce wall support, we expect that people with progressive racial attitudes, such as those who believe Latinos and immigrants face high levels of discrimination, will express greater opposition to the wall. Similarly, we expect those who acknowledge white privilege will also be more likely to oppose the wall. We expect these factors to moderate support for the wall because we believe these people will be more likely to identify the symbolism of the wall as Othering and excluding immigrants, Latinos, and nonwhites. Likewise, we believe individuals who recognize the levels of discrimination that Latinos and immigrants face are likely to be more capable of calculating the potential harmful consequences of building a wall in terms of which groups it will target and who will experience its negative effects.

2.8 Public Support for the Wall

To measure support for a border wall, we asked respondents, "Do you support or oppose the construction of a border wall along the entire US–Mexico border?" Answer choices included: "Strongly Support," "Somewhat Support," "Somewhat Oppose," and "Strongly Oppose." Overall, we find an overwhelming majority of people oppose the wall. The data reveals that only 18 percent of those surveyed strongly support the wall, compared to 53 percent who strongly oppose its construction. If we combine both levels of opposition (strongly and somewhat oppose), 67 percent of people surveyed oppose the wall. This aggregate total is similar to contemporary public polls, such as Gallup.

A very different picture of attitudes emerges if we examine partisan and ideological differences. Support among Republicans is markedly higher than that of non-Republicans: nearly 50 percent of Republicans strongly support the wall, and another 31 percent somewhat support it, for a total of nearly 81 percent support. Among non-Republican respondents (independents and Democrats), 71 percent strongly oppose the wall, and another 16 percent somewhat oppose the wall. Thus, nearly 88 percent of non-Republicans express opposition to the wall, which is close in total percentage to the percentage of Republicans who support it. It is also worth noting that the degree of strong opposition expressed by non-Republicans is considerably stronger than the degree of strong support among Republicans, as indicated by a much greater percentage of non-Republicans expressing strong opposition.

Comparing Republicans directly to Democrats and independents, the difference in levels of support is also substantial. While 81 percent of Republicans support the wall, only 7 percent of Democrats and 40 percent of independents express support for it. Although ideology and partisanship are related, they do not measure precisely the same thing. Comparing support across ideologies, we observe similar levels of polarization, with 80 percent of conservatives expressing support for the wall compared to only 6 percent of liberals and 41 percent of moderates. In sum, Republican partisanship and conservative ideology are key factors explaining support for the border wall. These results are important, because they indicate that opinion on the wall is significantly divided by party and ideology and is indicative of high levels of polarization. Unfortunately, this gap in public attitudes creates conditions in which it is difficult to imagine people from both sides of the aisle coming together in agreement or any sort of compromise.

Our statistical results examine how different factors influence wall support and the degree of their influence (see Figure 1). Confirming our theoretical expectations on partisanship, threat, and racial attitudes, we find that several crucial factors drive support for the wall. The role of partisanship is undeniable and is associated with a 25 percentage-point increase in support of the wall. Feeling culturally threatened by Latin American immigrants has a similar relationship, driving a 24 percentage-point increase. Likewise, those who feel demographically threatened are also more likely to support the wall, with a nearly 13 percentage-point increase in support. Support also increases among those who are most racially resentful (12 percentage-point increase). Not surprisingly, people who watch Fox News are more likely to support the wall (13 percentage-point change). Lastly, people who hold the most negative perceptions of the economy are also more likely to support the wall.

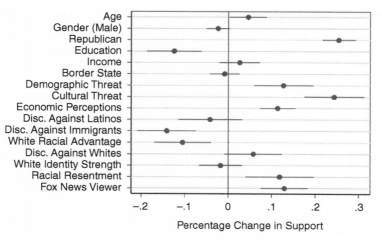

Note: Coefficient plot (OLS) indicating percentage point change in support for the relevant outcome. Lines indicate 95 percent confidence intervals.

Figure 1 Support for the wall

A few factors are shown to significantly reduce wall support. Consistent with prior work showing a moderating impact of higher education on support for restrictive immigration policies, we find that education results in a 12 percentage-point decrease in wall support. Progressive racial attitudes, such as whether people acknowledge white privilege (10 percentage-point decrease) or recognize the high levels of discrimination that immigrants face (14 percentage-point decrease), also reduce wall support. These results are consistent with our theoretical expectations.[9]

2.9 Public Perceptions of Wall Effectiveness

As noted earlier in this section, states have historically justified the need to build walls as an attempt to stop drugs (Vallet 2016), terrorism (Brown 2017; Longo 2018), and clandestine migrants (Hasner & Wittenberg 2015; Longo 2018). Broadly grouped, these can all be described as attempts to stop illicit flows (Andreas 2000a); countries often root their arguments in this security perspective. Other scholars have suggested that states build walls primarily for economic security (Hasner & Wittenberg 2015; Carter & Poast 2017). The

---

[9] Perceptions of the discrimination Latinos face does not result in a statistically significant relationship in any of our statistical models. Given the level of racialization Latinos face around immigration (Chavez 2008; Masuoka & Junn 2013; Zepeda-Millan 2014), this is surprising. It may be, however, that the public sees these policies as most directly impacting immigrants, whether Latino or non-Latino.

narrative of an uncontrolled mass of immigrants entering the United States through the US–Mexico border has dominated public debates and media depictions of immigration (Chavez 2001). Chavez notes that this metaphor manifests in various ways, including depicting immigrants as a massive overpowering "flood" or large groups of immigrants ready to cross the border in a line that extends to infinity (2001). He contends this imagery is very powerful in shaping public discourse.

In his first presidential address from the Oval Office in 2019, Trump repeatedly spoke of immigrant flows as a crisis and doubled down on drawing connections between immigrants and crime, drugs, and gangs. He said, "the Southern border is a pipeline for vast quantities of illegal drugs," and that it is necessary to "stop the criminal gangs, drug smugglers, and human traffickers" (Taylor 2019). Later that year, when facing a lack of Congressional funding for the wall, Trump resorted to declaring a national emergency in order to allow him to reallocate funds from other sources, such as the military. He defended his declaration by emphasizing an "unprecedented surge in the number of alien families arriving at the southern border," and made the case for wall funding by arguing that "securing our border is vital to ensuring the safety of the American people" (Trump 2019). It is clear that Trump's public rhetoric is an attempt to boost public support for the wall and justify its construction; in doing so, he has frequently relied on all three of the standard rationales for wall building – drugs, terrorism, and undocumented immigrants.

Separate from whether any of these claims are true or accurate, of which there is dubious evidence, we are interested in whether the public thinks a border wall is likely to impact any of these factors. We know little about public perceptions of the wall's projected effectiveness, especially in light of skepticism about its efficiency among experts (Frazee & Barajas 2019). If people do not think walls are effective for the reasons governments and leaders say we need them, then why do they continue to support their construction? We suggest that Trump's border wall acts as an important cultural symbol against immigrants and immigration. In this sense, we contribute to a long line of literature suggesting that border walls are used as an Othering device and tool for division (Newman & Passi 1998; Dear 2013; Vallet & David 2014).

We directly test these justifications for the border wall by asking respondents three questions about its potential effectiveness. All questions had the same answer choices of "Strongly Agree," "Somewhat Agree," "Somewhat Disagree," and "Strongly Disagree." First, we asked, "Do you agree or disagree that the construction of a border wall along the US–Mexico border will stop illegal immigration?"[10] Second, we used a similar question wording but asked whether respondents thought the wall would "stop terrorists from entering the country." Finally, respondents were asked whether the border wall would "stop illegal drugs from entering the country."

When examining general beliefs on the wall's effectiveness, it is clear that there is deep skepticism. Across all three dimensions, a minority of respondents indicate they agree that the border wall will be effective. Only 28 percent indicate they believe the wall will be effective in stopping undocumented immigrants; just 23 percent believe it will stop the flow of illegal drugs; and only 20 percent believe it will be effective against terrorism. It does not appear, then, that the public is swayed by Trump's justifications for the wall.

The results are deeply divided by partisan affiliation, with Republicans showing stronger belief in the wall's effectiveness, though they still express considerable doubt across all three dimensions. Among Republicans, 68 percent expressed some level of agreement that the wall would stop undocumented immigrants, which means nearly a third do not agree that the wall will be effective for this purpose. Perceptions of effectiveness are even lower for drugs (56 percent) and terrorism (49 percent), with half of Republicans indicating they do not believe it will be effective for these purposes. If we compare Republican perceptions of effectiveness to Republican support for the wall as a policy, there is a substantial disjuncture. Over 80 percent of Republicans expressed approval for building a wall, with 50 percent expressing strong approval. By contrast, only 20 percent of Republicans strongly agreed the wall would be effective in stopping undocumented immigration, 13 percent strongly agreed it would stop drugs, and 10 percent strongly agreed it would stop terrorism. We argue, then, that support for the wall among Republicans, despite their limited belief in its effectiveness, is rooted in the symbolic power of the wall to serve as an exclusionary device.

Our statistical models examining the factors driving perceptions of wall effectiveness reveal the same patterns as our models explaining wall support (see Figures 2a–c). The most consistent factors influencing attitudes toward wall effectiveness across all three dimensions are whether the respondent is Republican, feels culturally or demographically threatened, is worried about the economy, and is a Fox News viewer. The substantive impact of these factors is not consistent across all three dimensions, however. The largest substantive effects are observed when we analyze attitudes toward whether the wall will stop undocumented immigration. Here, we find that cultural threat (22 percentage-point change), demographic threat (12 percentage-point change), partisanship (17 percentage-point change), and whether someone is a Fox News viewer

---

[10] On question wording, see Section 1.7, "Note on Terminology."

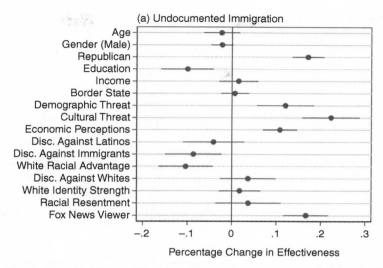

Figure 2a Beliefs in the effectiveness of the wall to stop undocumented immigration

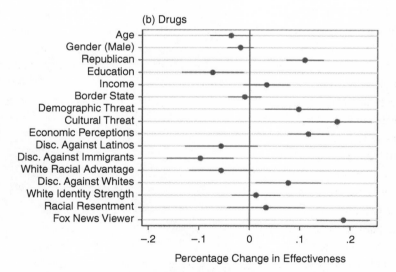

Figure 2b Beliefs in the effectiveness of the wall to stop drugs

(16 percentage-point change) all substantially increase whether a person will agree the wall will be effective. Even more moderate associations for factors like economic perceptions (10 percentage-point change) remain sizeable.

On drugs and terrorism, the impact of various factors is not quite as strong on perceptions of effectiveness. Cultural threat remains a key factor for both,

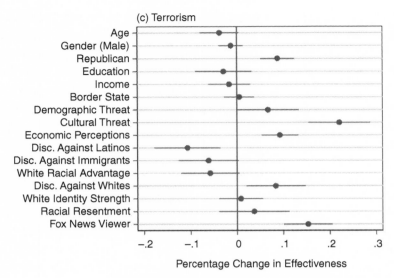

(c) Terrorism

Percentage Change in Effectiveness

Note to Figures 2a–c: Coefficient plots (OLS) indicating percentage
point change in beliefs about effectiveness for relevant outcome.
Lines indicate 95 percent confidence intervals.

Figure 2c Beliefs in the effectiveness of the wall to stop terrorism

associated with a 17 percentage-point increase on the drug question and
a 22 percentage-point change on the terrorism question. Likewise, being a Fox
News viewer has a substantial impact, with an 18 percentage-point increase on
perceptions of drug effectiveness and a 15 percentage-point change on terrorism
effectiveness. Party plays less of a role, with more modest 9 and 11 percentage-
point increases, respectively. Both demographic threat and economic perceptions
also play a much weaker role in explaining attitudes toward drug and terrorism
effectiveness, with both associated with around a 10 percentage-point change.
Overall, results across the three effectiveness models underscore partisan differences and the key impact of both cultural and demographic threat, economic
perceptions, and conservative news media on the public's beliefs.

2.10 Conclusion

According to Jones (2017), US border fortification policies are implemented to
appease the country's white citizenry (viii). While the elected officials who push
for these laws do tend to be white, our findings show that a relatively small
proportion of white respondents strongly support a border wall or believe it
would be effective. While opinions on the wall are deeply polarized along party
and ideological lines, with fervent support from Republicans and conservatives,
other factors that influence support include perceptions of the economy and

consumption of the right-wing views broadcasted on Fox News. However, as our results also show, racial attitudes greatly influence wall support. In line with the spirit of Jones's argument, our findings demonstrate that whites who fear the cultural impact of Latino immigrants, who harbor racially resentful sentiments, and who feel demographically threatened by people of color becoming the majority of the US population are significantly more likely to support Trump's plan to build a wall on the US–Mexico border. These xenophobic mindsets are also associated with believing a border fortification will achieve the president's promised results.

Racial attitudes thus matter when it comes to opinions about a wall along the US–Mexico divide. Drawing on prior scholarship, we have argued that border bulwarks not only serve as markers of state sovereignty, they also attempt to symbolically preserve an imagined or desired national racial homogeneity, are instruments of division, and are tools for the Othering of foreignness. Our empirical results corroborate these contentions, demonstrating that while the majority of whites do not support a border fortification or think it would work, the most racist ones do. Thus, our findings suggest that Trump's wall is less about sound policy or a reflection of the public's desires than it is about appealing to the most racially bigoted segments of the country.

3 Child Detention and Family Separation

> We are in a metal cage with 20 other teenagers with babies and young children. We have one mat we need to share with each other. It is very cold . . . Sometimes it is so crowded we cannot find a place to sleep . . . The lights are [on] all of the time.
> – Child detainee, 2019

> At least during the internment of Japanese-Americans, I and other children were not stripped from our parents. We were not pulled screaming from our mothers' arms.
> – George Takei, World War II internment camp survivor, 2019

To help build a barrier in the hope of deterring unsanctioned crossings, in 1945 the Border Patrol received 4,500 feet of chain-link fencing that the federal government had previously used in an internment camp.[11] "The wires and posts that had imprisoned Japanese Americans during World War II were dug up from the deserts ... and driven into the sands of the US–Mexico border to keep Mexicans out" (Lytle Hernandez, 2010: 130). This event eerily foreshadowed not only the fortressing of America described in Section 2 but also its connections to the country's time-honored tradition of confining racialized migrants and their children in chain-link camps and cages (Kahn 1996; Dow 2005).

With this history in mind, no irony was lost when in 2019 the Trump administration announced it would hold over a thousand unaccompanied migrant children in one of the same locations that had served as a World War II Japanese-American internment camp (Wu 2019). These actions were part of the president's "zero-tolerance" detention and family separation policy, which sought to punish and deter Central American migrants attempting to follow both US and international asylum application laws.

This section examines public opinion on current child migrant caging and family separation. As we will see, a detention system whose history is riddled with racism continues to be supported by xenophobic sentiments.

3.1 Why Detention?

Various scholars argue that immigrant detention can be understood "as a mechanism of social control for unpopular and powerless persons," mainly undocumented migrants and asylum seekers (Welch, 1996: 178; Colman & Kocher, 2011: 234). According to Coutin (2010), neoliberal globalization has created economies that are both dependent on undocumented labor and that use detention and deportation as key tools to discipline these workers (201). As De Genova (2017) explains, it is the detainability of noncitizens – their susceptibility to detention – deriving from "their distinctive legal vulnerability," that

---

[11] Epigraphs are from Koerner (2019) and Takei (2018).

facilitates their subordination "as a highly exploitable workforce" (166). Hence, Escobar (2016) asserts that detention in the United States is part of a larger racialized "neoliberal arrangement, where the capturing and warehousing" of some Latino migrants disciplines many more of them into serving as "ideal neoliberal laborers – flexible workers with minimal rights" (28).

The rise of neoliberalism has coincided with the expansion of migrant detention (part of a broader penal turn) and the exacerbation of economic insecurities in both developed and underdeveloped countries (Flynn & Flynn, 2017: 121). Flynn (2017) explains that on top of leading to the displacement and international migration of laborers from the global South, neoliberal policies have resulted in cuts to social welfare benefits and job insecurity for workers in places like the United States and Western Europe (174–176). He contends that because these rich nations remain committed to global capitalism, and thus are not interested in addressing the root causes of migration, they respond to nationalist calls for nativist policies through ineffective but electorally popular efforts such as detention and deportation (177).

Mountz et al. (2012) underscore that capital also responds to the perceived threat of migrants through the confluence of state and corporate economic and political incentives that promote detention, creating what is known as the "immigration industrial complex" (529; Fernandes 2007). The deindustrialization that decimated many local and state governments across the United States, for example, has led several of them to turn to immigrant detention as a revenue-generating strategy (Conlon & Hiemstra, 2014: 336). ICE frequently contracts with these locales, who then subcontract out to private prisons, leading to 65 percent of the agency's detainees being held in for-profit facilities today (Ryo & Peacock, 2018: 7; Garcia Hernandez, 2019: 15). Private prison companies make billions from these lucrative financial arrangements, achieved through campaign contributions, lobbying, and the actual writing of punitive immigration legislation (Golash-Boza 2009; Ackerman & Furman 2013; Collingwood et al. 2018). The corporate crafting of anti-immigrant policies is particularly effective at moneymaking, in that the more the lives of immigrants are criminalized – from local anti–day laborer ordinances to federal policies like Secure Communities – the more likely immigrants are to be arrested and detained, insuring a larger and continuous revenue stream for private prison companies (Ackerman & Furman, 2013: 254–255; Doty & Wheatley, 2013: 253).

Other scholars argue that immigrant detention also serves symbolic functions, one of which is the performance of state power, meant to reinforce national sovereignty through the incarceration – and eventual expulsion – of unwanted foreigners (Coutin, 2010: 207; Mainwaring & Silverman, 2017: 29).

Detention operates as a "strategic spectacle of enforcement" intended to both deter future migrants and reassure anxious citizens that their government is addressing their "racialized security concerns" (Martin, 2012a: 325–330; Hiemstra, 2014: 574–575). The selective targeting of specific minority groups for detention (e.g., Latinos) has the effect of confirming and sustaining racialized suspicions of criminality, justifying their confinement and bolstering support for enhancing immigration enforcement measures (De Genova, 2007: 434–435; Mainwaring & Silverman, 2017: 31).

In this fashion, despite the United States' "family values" and "reunification" rhetoric, when migrant families are apprehended they are often framed as threats to the national order, necessitating their detention as a "crime prevention strategy" and their separation as a form of discipline and deterrence (Martin, 2012b: 873; Martin, 2017b: 358, 359). These concerns are not only racial but also gendered, in that the fertility of migrant women remains a source of great anxiety for those who fear the "browning of America" (Luibheid 2002; Chavez, 2008: 96). Accordingly, detention displays a government's power to distinguish those who are demographically desired as part of the nation from those who aren't. State narratives of detention produce and reify differences between citizens and racialized foreigners, as detainees are rhetorically and visually constructed as dangerous criminal and cultural "Others" who deserve to be castigated (Hiemstra, 2014: 584; Mainwaring & Silverman, 2017: 30).

This collective demonization dehumanizes migrants, allowing governments to exert their monopoly on violence against them (Cornelisse, 2010: 102). Consequently, detention camps have been described as permanent states of moral and legal exception (Agamben 1998) where detainees are distanced "from their humanity, and from the realization of that humanity by others" (Rajaram, 2003: 7). Violence against detainees becomes routine and normalized, allowing many citizens to go about their daily lives without blinking an eye after seeing images of, or reading stories about, migrant family separation or sick and hungry brown babies locked in cages.

Below, we offer a concise overview of key legislative actions that made the latter phenomenon into official US policy.

3.2 Immigrant Detention Policy

The legal and ideological foundations of the US government's immigrant detention system can be traced back to its Native-American removal campaigns and fugitive slave laws, as well as multiple anti-Chinese court cases and Japanese-American internment (Kanstroom 2007; Silverman 2010; Hernandez 2019). In order to establish a more "humane administration of immigration laws," however, in the 1950s – when Europeans were still the majority of immigrants coming to the United States – the government virtually abolished its immigrant detention system (Garcia Hernandez, 2019: 47). Up until the 1980s, incarceration was not a major feature of immigration enforcement, since most people suspected of immigration violations were quickly released on bond or parole (Macias-Rojas, 2016: 56). But in the late 1970s and early 1980s, thousands of Haitian and Cuban asylum seekers began arriving on US shores, sparking a "racial panic" (Hernandez, 2019: 76). The "Haitian-Cuban Crisis" overwhelmed immigration officials and caught President Carter by surprise, leading him to spend his final year in the White House confining asylum seekers in various types of facilities in the hope of deterring more from coming (Loyd & Mountz, 2018: 22).

Upon entering office, President Reagan wasted no time in dealing with this "racial panic" by "initiating the first massive expansion of detention" through mandating the confinement of all asylum seekers (Hiemstra, 2019: 53–54). His primary targets were Haitians and Cubans, but quickly expanded to include Central Americans fleeing right-wing dictators whom his administration supported (Simon, 1998: 583). Reagan's shift to mandatory detention immediately filled existing facilities beyond capacity (Dunn, 1996: 46–47; Hiemstra, 2019: 54). As a result, the president opened several new detention centers, one of which was the first "specifically designed to imprison children and babies" (Kahn, 1996: 117; see also Schrag 2020).[12] Kids in detention were held in atrocious conditions with no bond and were stripped and body-cavity searched before and after each meeting with their legal representatives (Kahn, 1996: 15). Families and unaccompanied minors were also held in Red Cross camps and "bare-boned" tent shelters along the US–Mexico border (Schriro, 2017a: 29).

Reagan increased the budget for detention and deportations by 191 percent to $1.28 million (Dunn, 1996: 45) and enacted three laws that helped fuel the expansion of detention. While his racially coded "war on drugs" was raging, the president signed the Anti-Drug Abuse Acts of 1986 and 1988. The former allowed the detention and deportation of noncitizens for even minor drug-related offenses, while the latter created the concept and mandated the detention of "aggravated felons" (Ryo, 2019: 102). Initially, an "aggravated felony" consisted of any one of three serious crimes – murder, drug trafficking, and weapons trafficking – but its definition has since been expanded to include over thirty types of offences, including many that are only misdemeanors for citizens (American Immigration Council, 2016). Reagan additionally signed IRCA, which criminalized previously noncriminal actions such as working while undocumented and consequently substantially augmented the pool of detainable migrants (Inda 2013).

---

[12] See Schrag (2020) for a recently released and detailed history of child detention.

George H. W. Bush continued these trends with a new – but equally racially charged – focus on "criminal aliens" that disproportionally targeted undocumented Mexicans (Dunn, 1996: 70, 72; Hernandez, 2019: 77), who now comprise the vast majority of detainees (Bosworth & Kaufman, 2011: 435). Through several policies, including the 1990 Immigration Act and the 1990 Crime Control Act, Bush increased funding for and enabled the confinement of immigrants awaiting the outcome of their deportation cases, as well as of asylum seekers whose claims were denied (Bosworth & Kaufman, 2011: 442; Garcia Hernandez, 2014: 1368). Bush also used the US military base in Guantanamo Bay as an offshore detention site with segregated "camps," including units specifically for families and one known as "kid jail" (Loyd & Mountz, 2018: 154).

After the initial "refugee crisis" subsided, the number of individuals detained significantly declined throughout the 1980s and early 1990s (Dunn, 1996: 187). Between 1994 and 2000, however, the average daily population of detainees ballooned from 6,785 to 19,458 (Reyes 2018). Why? During the early 1990s, a rising unemployment rate and events from California's Proposition 187 to the Oklahoma City bombing (carried out by a white military veteran but initially blamed on Arab terrorists) fueled economic anxieties and a racist backlash against noncitizens (Silverman, 2010: 12; Chacon, 2014: 621–625). In this context, in 1996, President Clinton signed two laws – the Antiterrorism and Effective Death Penalty Act (AEDPA) and the Illegal Immigration Reform and Immigrant Responsibility Act (IIRIRA) – that enhanced the push to confine migrants and criminalize their daily lives (Loyd & Mountz, 2018: 175).

AEDPA, for instance, broadened the list of crimes defined as aggravated felonies and "expanded the types of offenses (beyond aggravated felonies) that trigger mandatory detention" (Ryo & Peacock, 2018: 8). IIRIRA was even more punishing. Among its numerous punitive provisions, the law continued to increase the number of offenses considered aggravated felonies, mandated detention for noncitizens convicted of certain misdemeanors and for individuals subject to expedited removal, and greatly limited judicial discretion. In addition, IIRIRA increased funding for detention beds, made deportation for immigrants with "criminal" records retroactive, enabled the possibility of indefinite detention, permitted the use of "secret evidence" as a justification for detention, and created a program known as 287(g) that allowed local law enforcement officers to work with immigration agents (Macias-Rojas, 2016: 9, 61–63; Wong, 2017: 83; Juarez et al., 2018: 75–76).

Under Clinton, the practice of detaining asylee families and children also persisted (Loyd & Mountz, 2018: 169–171), and, as during the 1980s, reports of child abuse in detention throughout the 1990s were rampant because there were no regulations for the confinement of migrant minors during this period (Kahn,

1996: 117–118). But after a decade-long lawsuit (*Flores vs. Meese*), in 1997, immigration authorities agreed to a settlement known as the Flores Agreement, or Flores. Flores established national standards for the detention of minors, which included the provisions of sufficient food, water, access to restrooms, educational programs, and emergency medical care; standards for treatment such as supervision, protection from unrelated adults, ventilation, and temperature control; and requirements for the release of migrant children within three to five days, with an extension of up to twenty days in times of "influxes" and "emergencies" (Kandel, 2017: 3; Schriro, 2017b: 454; Human Rights First, 2018).

According to Hing (2019), the Flores "guidelines require that juveniles be held in the 'least restrictive setting appropriate to their age and special needs, generally in a non-secure facility licensed to care for dependent, as opposed to delinquent, minors.'" They also mandate that "juveniles be released from custody without unnecessary delay to a parent, licensed program, or alternatively, an adult seeking custody deemed appropriate by the responsible government agency'" (2019: 96). One immediate effect of the Flores Agreement was that facilities detaining families, because they held children, now had to meet the standards set by Flores. In response, the US government opened its first permanent family detention center in March 2001 (Martin, 2017a: 41). Nevertheless, since Flores's inception, criticisms over its violation and inadequate implementation have been widespread (Kandel, 2017: 4).

Scholars agree that 9/11 was another key catalyst to the expansion of the US immigrant detention system. Under the guise of national security, President George W. Bush signed several significant pieces of legislation – including the 2001 USA Patriot Act, the 2002 Homeland Security Act, the 2005 CLEAR Act, and the 2005 REAL ID Act, among others – that critically expanded the administration's power and resources to detain more migrants, including indefinitely and without charge (Hiemstra, 2019: 56–57). Before this period, at-capacity detention centers regularly let out migrants who had no prior convictions on recognizance, the so-called "catch and release" policy (Macias-Rojas, 2016: 69). Attempting to put an end to this practice, the Department of Homeland Security enacted several strategies, including "Operation Endgame" and the Secure Border Initiative, that laid out a plan to capture and deport all "removable" immigrants, boosted the budgets and number of immigration agents, and upped detention bed space by eight thousand a year (Wong 2015: 120; Hiemstra, 2019: 56–57). Just as significant was Bush's post-9/11 activation of IIRIRA's underutilized 287(g) clause. Federal-local police partnerships under 287(g) enhanced the ability of the laws just discussed to be implemented at the local level by essentially creating a racial dragnet that has greatly contributed to the post-9/11 upsurge in Latino immigrant detention

(Coleman, 2012: 167). These enforcement practices help explain why, despite the total number of interior and border apprehensions declining during G. W. Bush's presidency, the average daily population of detainees jumped from 20,429 in 2001 to 31,771 by 2008, a nearly 56 percent increase (Chacon, 2013: 88; Ryo, 2019: 101; Reyes 2018).

Families were particularly adversely affected by policy and enforcement changes made under G. W. Bush. In 2004 and 2005, for example, DHS expanded its application of expedited removal to include many "families who had not been subject to mandatory detention" (Martin, 2017a: 41). In addition, the pre-9/11 releasing or detaining of families as units was "largely abandoned," and parents were now frequently split from their children upon apprehension. Outraged by these actions, the House Appropriations Committee directed the DHS to end this practice and begin releasing families or using alternatives to detention (Schriro, 2017a: 30). Instead, the DHS recommissioned "a former medium-security prison as a stand-alone" detention center for migrant family units (Garcia Hernandez, 2019: 145). Reports of horrific conditions and abuses at this and other detention centers continued under G. W. Bush (Hing 2019).

During Obama's first year in office, while Congress instituted a detention "bed mandate" of 33,400 (Macias-Rojas, 2016: 73), the president ordered DHS to undertake "a comprehensive assessment of detention policy and practices," with one of the goals being "reducing reliance on detention" (Schriro, 2017a: 32). Initial reforms included closing the complaint-ridden Hutto detention center and releasing many of the families held there, as well as reducing family detention bed space from 384 to only 84 (Schriro, 2017b: 457). In fact, from 2009 through 2014, instead of detaining, "ICE returned to its previous policy of issuing Notices to Appear to most families" (Martin, 2017a: 42). Under Obama, 85 to 90 percent of unaccompanied children were also freed from federal custody to sponsors (Chen & Gill, 2015: 118; Chishti & Hipsman, 2015: 101). Yet reports of the maltreatment of detainees persisted, including cases of family separation due to the detention or deportation of parents (Applied Research Center 2011; Enchautegui & Menjivar 2015).

The most notable incidents related to detention under Obama began in 2014. Fleeing violence and poverty in Central America, approximately 69,000 unaccompanied minors and 68,000 family units (adults traveling with children) – many of whom sought asylum – were apprehended at the southern border, with a similar number arriving in 2016 (Chishti & Hipsman, 2015: 95–96; Nakamura 2016). These events caught the administration off guard and with limited detention space to house the vulnerable migrants. As the number of migrants at the border increased, the president went from attempting to roll back family detention and discussing the crisis as "an urgent humanitarian situation," to framing it as a "threat to national security" that necessitated confinement as a deterrence strategy (Chishti & Hipsman, 2015: 103; Schriro, 2017b: 460–463). In response, although the administration convinced Congress to approve $750 million in development aid for Central America, created an "in-country processing program" allowing Central American children to apply for family reunification from their home countries, and launched a $1.8 million program to provide legal representation to unaccompanied minors, it also began "fast-tracking" court hearings, stopped releasing most families from detention, and opened several new family detention facilities (Chishti & Hipsman, 2015: 103–104; Schriro, 2017b: 463; Hing, 2019: 283, 299). Perhaps because most of these immigrant children were released to sponsors, or merely revealing partisan hypocrisy, images of kids inside chain-link cages during this period drew few criticisms from Democrats (Lovato 2019). Nonetheless, in toto, despite the average daily population of detainees growing only slightly from 32,098 to 34,376 throughout his presidency, between 2009 and 2016 Obama expanded family detention capacity from 84 to 3,750 beds (Schriro, 2017a: 32; Reyes 2018).

Cumulatively, the aforementioned policies have resulted in the United States having the largest immigrant detention system in the world (Garcia Hernandez, 2019: 11). How effective these policies have been in achieving their stated aims is the topic we take up in Section 3.3.

3.3 Does Detention Work?

If the goal is to make detention so excruciating that asylum seekers and other detainees give up on fighting their cases, then qualitative evidence suggests that, at least on some occasions, this policy is effective (Golash-Boza, 2015: 214–216). As Martin (2012a) explains, "Fed up with long detention stays, some detainees chose to sign voluntary deportation orders and forego legitimate claims" rather than continue suffering in confinement (327). Unfortunately, it is nearly impossible to estimate how widespread this phenomenon is. That said, if the aim is to deter future migrants from coming – as every president from Carter to Trump has claimed – then detention and family separation appear to be ineffective.

According to Ryo (2019), research has generally found that detention shows "no evidence of deterrence" (109). Statistical studies, for example, reveal that while being the victim of a crime increases an individual's intention to emigrate, being aware of the possible dangers awaiting them in the US detention system does not serve as a deterrent (Hiskey et al. 2018: 430). In fact, survey research suggests that rather than discourage, detention has had a "caging effect" on many migrants, in that it has disrupted their seasonal migration flows, increased familial and social ties to the United States, and diminished their chances of returning to their home countries (Slack et al. 2015: 110; Cox & Goodman 2018; Wong 2018). In other words, just as walls fail to deter desperate migrants from crossing, so too does detention.

3.4 Trump's "Zero-Tolerance" Policy

In early 2017, again due to surging violence in Central America (which has among the highest murder rates in the world), unaccompanied minors and families seeking asylum began fleeing to Mexico and the United States. In an attempt to avoid abuses that repeatedly occur when migrating alone, they chose to travel in large groups – dubbed "migrant caravans" – for safety. A few months later, the Trump administration began secretly piloting a "zero-tolerance" program that detained migrant families and referred parents (usually mothers) for criminal prosecution, even if it meant separating them from their children, who were sent to detention centers and shelters elsewhere (Hirschfeld Davis & Shear, 2019: 253; Lee, 2019: 331–332). As some DHS officials bluntly described the practice, "harm to children is being deliberately used for its deterrent effect" (Hirschfeld Davis & Shear, 2019: 260). In April 2018, spewing racist stereotypes of Latino migrant criminality, Trump declared that "more must be done to enforce our laws and to protect our country from the dangers of releasing detained aliens into our communities." Hours later, believing media coverage of kids being stripped from their parents would discourage more asylum seekers from coming, Attorney General Jeff Sessions officially announced "a policy of zero tolerance for illegal border crossings" (Hirschfeld Davis & Shear, 2019: 254–255).

While family separation had occurred under previous administrations on individual bases, no American president before Trump had made it official public policy and enthusiastically practiced it on a mass scale. The results of this new program were that in just a few months, more than 5,400 children were taken from their parents and reclassified as unaccompanied minors, the youngest only four months old (Dickerson 2019; Associated Press 2019). Parents were often deported without their children, who were forcibly kept behind by the US government. Trump's family separation policy was immediately condemned not only by migrant rights activists and professional organizations like the American Academy of Pediatrics, but also by many news outlets, the United Nations, the Pope, and even the conservative US Chamber of Commerce (Hirschfeld Davis & Shear, 2019: 277; Wadhia, 2019: 110).

Arguably in response to the public uproar over images of screaming babies being pulled from their mothers' arms and crying children put in kennel-like cages, after several months Trump publicly issued an executive order claiming to end family separation. According to Hirschfeld Davis and Shear (2019), this retreat marked "the first real moment since taking office that Trump had backed down on a major immigration initiative" (278). Despite a federal judge ordering the Trump administration to immediately reunite families, however, the zero-tolerance policy proved "even more cruel and inhumane than we thought," given that the federal government "lost track" and still cannot identify the locations of thousands of the children it took from their parents (Gerstein & Hesson 2018; Montini 2019). Moreover, the president's attacks on migrant children and families have persisted. Trump has not only attempted to end Flores so that migrant children can be detained indefinitely, his administration has violated its own executive order by continuing to separate hundreds of families (Gonzales 2019; Silva 2019).

With this history in mind, in the following sections we describe the contemporary conditions of detainee confinement and examine public opinion on family separation and child detention.

3.5 Conditions of Immigrant Detention

In 2015, the ACLU, the National Immigration Law Center, and the American Immigration Council brought a class-action lawsuit on behalf of migrants challenging the inhumane conditions in detention facilities in the Tucson sector of the US Border Patrol. In *Doe vs. Wolf* (formerly *Doe vs. Nielsen, Doe vs. Kelly,* and *Doe vs. Johnson*), the plaintiffs charged that these practices were in violation of US Customs and Border Protection's own policies and the Constitution. Extensive interviews with migrants confirmed that they were held for lengthy periods of time in freezing-cold and filthy cells with limited access to showers, adequate meals, and water, sleeping on concrete floors under Mylar blankets, with limited to no access to health care or lawyers, held incommunicado, and deprived of basic hygiene supplies such as soap, sufficient toilet paper, menstrual products, diapers, and showers (Marquez-Avila, 2019; American Immigration Council, n.d.). Despite this ongoing litigation and the still-standing Flores Agreement, poor conditions in immigrant detention facilities housing adults and children continue to persist today.

During 2018 and 2019, there were widespread reports, some from Flores monitors, of extremely deplorable conditions in detention facilities housing children, including severe overcrowding, poor hygiene, poor temperature conditions, limited health care, and little access to essential items including clothing, diapers, food, and baby formula (Dickerson 2019; Long & Mukherjee 2019). While detention in these holding facilities is supposed to be temporary, children were being held far longer than the seventy-two hours usually allowed under Flores. Detailed reports, videos, and audio recordings of the poor conditions generated significant media attention, public outcry, and eventual backlash (Smith & Phillips 2018). The public debate focused on whether kids should be in cages and detained at all, whether better policy options existed, and what accommodations and rights children should have while in detention.

In June 2019, the US House of Representatives and Senate passed versions of a border aid bill aiming to provide $4.5 billion in funding to improve conditions in these facilities (Cochrane 2019; Willis 2019a). The House version focused on funds for the Department of Human and Health Services ($2.9 billion) to provide legal services for children and relieve overcrowding. The bill included an additional $17 million for legal services and $20 million for ICE to fund both alternatives to detention centers (Willis 2019b) and greater oversight guidelines on the care of migrant children (Cochrane 2019). These provisions were strongly advocated for by members of the Congressional Hispanic Caucus and the Congressional Progressive Caucus as necessary safeguards to protect against any misdirection of funds away from the dire needs of the children. The House bill passed with support from only three Republican legislators. The Senate version, meanwhile, garnered support from eighty-four senators across party lines. This was likely due to the fact that it contained far fewer limitations on how the money could be spent by the Trump administration. Congress was so disturbed by the reported conditions in detention that in July it held a hearing called "Kids in Cages" to listen to direct testimony (Sachetti 2019). Two months later, reports revealed that child detainees continued to suffer from extremely poor conditions (Kanno-Youngs 2019).

Even during the deadly COVID-19 (coronavirus) pandemic, the Trump administration did not relent on attacking migrants or attempt to make dire detention conditions any safer. At the start of the virus' outbreak in the United States, only about 1 percent of detainees were tested, 60 percent of which were confirmed to be infected with the dangerous disease, including many children (Martin 2020; Montoya-Galvez 2020). For instance, in one shelter alone, thirty-seven migrant kids tested positive for COVID-19 (Moreno 2020). Nevertheless, Trump repeatedly refused to release child detainees to sponsors (O'Toole and Carcamo 2020). Instead, his administration deported more than 400 minors through creating "new rules" that "scrapped decades-long practices under laws meant to protect children from human trafficking and offer them a chance to seek asylum" (Hesson and Rosenberg 2020). During this period, Trump's ICE agents were also accused of trying to exploit the pandemic by "pressuring immigrant parents to agree to being separated from their children," which would have made them easier to deport (da Silva 2020).

3.6 Polling on Family Separation and Detention

We know little about public attitudes toward the detention of immigrant children and family separation. While there has been some polling starting in mid-2018, there is a dearth of published scholarship. We hope to fill this gap by closely examining public opinion toward child detention and separation, as well as the factors that drive support for and opposition to these policies.

A Quinnipiac Poll conducted in summer 2018 indicates that 66 percent of the public opposes family separation and 32 percent support it, with 91 percent of Democrats and 68 percent of independents expressing opposition (Quinnipac University 2018). The poll also found that 55 percent of Republicans support the policy of family separation. A poll conducted by Ipsos for NPR around the same time found similar levels of opposition to the policy (Ipsos 2018; Matthews 2018), as did polls conducted by CNN and CBS News in June 2018 (O'Neil 2018). This data confirm family separation is an unpopular policy. Additionally, while the majority of Republicans do support the policy (55 percent), their support is considerably weaker than their level of support for the border wall, for which over 80 percent of Republicans expressed support.

There is far less public polling on child detention. Questions on existing surveys ask whether children should be detained as a preferred policy solution in cases of potential family separation. The questions do not ask whether children should be detained at all, and answer choices are often quite complicated, conflating child detention with family separation. An Economist/YouGov Poll from June 2018, for example, asked people their preferred option in family separation; answer choices included releasing the children and holding families together (Economist/YouGov 2018; O'Neil 2018). This type of question wording is problematic, because not all child detention occurs in the context of family separation. Children can also arrive in the United States unaccompanied or be traveling with other relatives or adults. This question wording does not allow us to ascertain opinion toward child detention and family separation separately or to measure attitudes toward different types of policy solutions regarding children who are detained. We designed our measures of attitudes toward detention and family separation to overcome these shortcomings.

3.7 Measuring Attitudes toward Child Detention and Family Separation

We utilize media reports and eyewitness accounts from detainees, activists, political elites, lawyers, and doctors on the conditions of detention facilities to inform the design of our measures. Given the public outcry against family separation and child detention, we believe it is important to assess what people think is the best solution when children are detained by immigration authorities. Under Flores, children are supposed to be released to a parent or sponsor as soon as possible (Lind & Scott 2018). President Trump also suggested in a series of tweets in June 2018 that immigrants may simply be immediately deported and not have the opportunity to go through a legal process to determine if they are eligible to stay (Chicau & Lynch 2018). In the current system, children are often detained in holding cells and then transferred to either family detention centers or to child-specific facilities. Thus, we asked respondents, "What should be done when migrant children are detained by immigration authorities?" Respondents were given the answer choices of putting the children in an immigrant detention facility, releasing the children to a family member or sponsor, or deporting them.

Because of reports indicating scarce resources and poor conditions in detention, widespread criticism, and the requirements of Flores to provide a certain level of basic needs when children are detained, we were also interested in what rights and accommodations people believe children should have in detention. We asked, "When migrant children are detained and held in child detention facilities without a parent or adult family member, which of the following should they have access to?" Respondents were instructed to select all options they believed should apply from a long list with no restriction on the number of items checked. The list included medical care, personal hygiene products (for example: soap, toothbrush, toothpaste, diapers), adequate amounts of food and water, English courses, educational courses, outdoor time for play and exercise, psychological services, adequate sleeping accommodations such as a bed or mat, legal counsel/attorney, and adequate temperature control and ventilation. While it may seem that some or all of these items should be granted to all detainees as a matter of course, extensive research indicates that access to a significant proportion of these items is often limited in prisons and jails (Katz et al. 2003; Wilper et al. 2009), including immigrant detention facilities (Neeley 2008; Schiriro 2010; Ryo 2019). Indeed, some research suggests the state views severe conditions in imprisonment as a deterrent despite limited empirical evidence that it works (Chen & Shapiro 2007; Raaijmakers et al. 2017). With regard to immigrant detention, for years there have been reports of freezing-cold holding cells often referred to as *hieleras* or iceboxes (Redden 2014; Cantor 2015; Riva 2017), and limited access to basic hygiene, food, medical services, and legal services (Phillips et al. 2006; Ryo & Peacock 2018).

While family separation has manifested in several different ways in the last three decades, the particular version espoused by the Trump administration in its zero-tolerance policy is unique, as is the dramatic increase in the number of child migrants detained (Sherman et al. 2019). As such, our survey item asked, "A new policy was recently implemented that says when families are caught crossing illegally into the United States through the US–Mexico border, the adults will be referred for criminal prosecution and their minor children will be separated from them and sent to a detention facility. Do you support or oppose this policy?" Answer choices ranged from "Strongly Support" to "Strongly Oppose."

In this section, our questions are centered on detention conditions and support for child detention and family separation policies. In Section 4, we will turn toward analyzing how information about the long-term harms of family separation and abuses that occur during child detention influence support for each policy.

3.8 Methodological Approach

We employ a similar approach to analyzing opinion toward children in detention and family separation as we used to examine support for the wall in Section 2. As a brief reminder, we utilize a host of background control variables in all of our statistical models, including gender, age, income, and education. Our primary explanatory variables are focused on cultural and demographic threat, racial attitudes, and partisanship. Specifically, we are interested in how demographic and cultural threat may increase support for child detention and family separation. Beyond threat, additional racial attitudes used in the statistical models include racial resentment; perceptions of discrimination toward Latinos, immigrants, and whites; strength of white identity; and perceptions of white privilege.[13] Given the large magnitude of differences in wall opinions by political party, we are again focused on both the impact of partisanship and the degree of polarization on support.

Our theoretical expectations on attitudes toward child detention and family separation are similar to our expectations on the factors that drove support for the border wall. Given polarization on immigration and the key role of party in explaining immigration attitudes (Abrajano & Hajnal 2015; Wong 2017; Wallace & Wallace 2020), we expect there to be significant partisan differences in attitudes toward child detention and family separation. We are less confident that Republican support for these policies will be as fervent as it is for the wall, because these policies were not critical components of Trump's campaign for the presidency. His rhetoric and action on these dimensions of immigration policy developed after he became president. Furthermore, child detention is not a subject he consistently returns to in his speeches or public rhetoric on immigration. Child detention and family separation also do not have the same ability to be distilled into a single symbol, as the border wall can. Images of these policies would necessarily have to portray the people who are harmed by

---

[13] A complete discussion of these variables is in section 2. Appendix A contains details on coding and question wording.

them, and this imagery might make some people feel uncomfortable or evoke a sense of moral outrage. Despite these qualifications to our expectations, we nonetheless expect broadly similar results as in Section 2, because child detention and family separation policies are consistent with other immigration enforcement policies that Republicans have generally supported.

We believe that racial attitudes and threat will play a significant role in explaining support for these policies. Family separation and child detention directly target immigrants and seek to create conditions that may deter people from migrating. We expect individuals who hold negative racial attitudes, such as high levels of racial resentment, to support these policies. People who feel threatened by demographic change and the cultural changes that result from immigration from Latin America would likely be more supportive of these policies, since they may see them as immigration enforcement measures that will reduce migration.

Similar to the wall, we also expect certain factors to moderate support for these policies. Individuals who recognize the discrimination Latinos and immigrants face may be less likely to support child detention and family separation because they realize that Latinos and immigrants will be harmed by them. We expect people who recognize white privilege to also be less supportive, because, again, they are cognizant that it is people of color who will experience the negative consequences of these policies. In sum, we expect that racial attitudes, threat, and partisanship will be the key drivers explaining opinions on family separation and child detention.

3.9 Public Support for Child Detention

Our results show that the public overwhelmingly rejects detaining children as the best policy option when children are in the custody of immigration authorities. When faced with the policy options of detention, releasing children to sponsors or family members, or deportation, the vast majority of those surveyed (82 percent) supported releasing immigrant children to sponsors or family members. Relatively few supported the removal of the children from the country via deportation (11 percent), and an even smaller proportion (6 percent) supported keeping children in immigrant detention facilities. Partisanship does play a role in these results, but Republicans' dominant policy choice was also releasing the children, with 57 percent selecting this option. Democrats overwhelmingly selected releasing children to a sponsor or family member (97 percent). A larger proportion of Republicans (27 percent) relative to the overall sample selected deportation, but detaining children remains the least popular choice, with only 16 percent of Republicans selecting this policy solution.

Turning to differences among those who feel a high level of cultural threat, we also see differences in opinion. We categorize high threat as those who responded somewhat, very, or extremely concerned, and respondents as low threat if they answered slightly or not at all concerned to our cultural threat question. Among people with low levels of threat, only 3 percent choose child detention, compared to 15 percent of people with high levels of threat. It is remarkable, however, that neither group selected child detention at a particularly high rate. If we compare support for the other two policy options, even greater differences emerge. Releasing children to family members or sponsors is the most preferred policy option among people with low levels of threat, at 92 percent compared to 55 percent of those with high levels. Only 5 percent of people with low levels of cultural threat express support for deportation, whereas 30 percent of those with high levels of cultural threat do. While we observe raw differences between some groups, all of these results confirm that child detention is quite unpopular as a policy.

The results also show, and the public believes, that the best policy option is the least restrictive. This viewpoint is consistent with what is required by Flores. The overwhelming majority of Democrats and the majority of Republicans support the least restrictive option, and only a very small percentage of people in each party support child detention. While a child detention policy has been implemented by the Trump administration, it lacks public support even among Trump's base. Because there is so much cohesion in opinion against detention, our analysis of this question is limited to overall levels of support of policy options, and we do not estimate full statistical models to examine the factors predicting variation in support.

3.10 Support for Rights during Detention

We find overwhelming evidence that the public supports access to a multitude of accommodations and rights for children detained by immigration authorities. This support largely transcends partisan differences. We asked respondents to choose elements from a list of items, rights, and experiences that they believed children being detained should have access to. The list included: medical care, personal hygiene products (for example: soap, toothbrush, toothpaste, diapers), adequate amounts of food and water, English courses, educational courses, outdoor time for play and exercise, psychological services, adequate sleeping accommodations such as a bed or mat, legal counsel/attorney, and adequate temperature control and ventilation. Figure 3 displays the raw results for each item and by partisanship. On six out of ten items, over 90 percent of respondents support detained children's access to that particular accommodation. These findings hold even when one examines partisan differences, with Republicans and Democrats overwhelmingly in support of access, scoring at least 85 percent

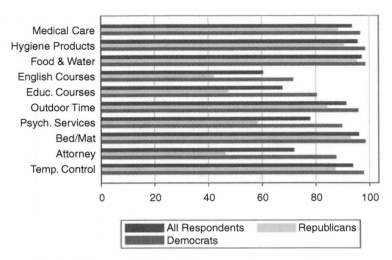

Figure 3 Support for rights in detention (overall and by party)

for each. These high levels of support may be explained as the public viewing access to these items as basic human rights that should be offered to any person in detention. People may be even more deeply motivated to support such a wide range of services and accommodations for a detained population of children. Some may feel uneasy about children being detained in the first place – as evidenced by our survey results – but particularly in conditions that are jail-like. They may view a lack of access to basic things, such as medical care and personal hygiene, as particularly unacceptable when children are involved. Regardless of the reason why people support access to these items, it is clear that the public does not support withholding access. But, as we know from reports on contemporary conditions inside detention facilities, many of these things – such as adequate food and water, temperature control, sleeping accommodations, medical care, and personal hygiene products – are not being supplied to children in detention.

Only in a few areas is there less than 90 percent support, and even these items were supported by almost two-thirds to three-quarters of respondents. The rights and services with the lowest levels of support include English courses (61 percent), education courses (68 percent), psychological services (78 percent), and legal services (72 percent). Partisanship accounts for much of this decreased support. On access to psychological services, for example, 90 percent of Democrats offer support, compared to only 58 percent of Republicans. Similar gaps are present for access to legal counsel/attorney, with support from 88 percent of Democrats versus 46 percent of Republicans. What these less-supported services and courses have in common is that they provide a means to increase skills or potential for greater advocacy by the detained child. This may be why some segments of the public are less supportive. An alternative explanation is that some may envision two tiers of rights and accommodations: one where basic needs are met, and a secondary tier of things that would be beneficial but are not critical.

To be clear, the detained population we are talking about is children, and they do not have the legal or intellectual capacity to represent themselves in complicated legal proceedings regarding their immigration status as minors. Thus, access to legal counsel is vital. The experience of being detained as a child can have long-term health effects from the trauma endured in these conditions (Linton et al. 2017; MacLean et al. 2019). Medical groups like the American Medical Association have advised Congress that children should not be held in these conditions and should have access to necessary medical and mental health services (Radwan 2019). While Republicans express less support for access to such services, there are strong, objective indications that such services are not secondary.

Despite lower levels of support across a few dimensions, our results lay bare extremely high levels of support for a wide-ranging set of rights and accommodations to be provided to children in detention. This amount of support, as well as cohesion in public opinion across party lines, is in conflict with the realities of contemporary child detention and with the government's position on what types of accommodations are required under Flores. In June 2019, in *Flores v. Barr*, the government argued that providing basic hygiene products, such as soap, toothbrushes, and toothpaste, to children while in detention was not necessarily required (Fernandez 2019). The judges reacted incredulously, questioning under what conditions these would not be considered basic items to provide (Fernandez 2019). Why, then, does Trump persist in providing such poor detention conditions when there has been widespread media outcry, Congressional hearings investigating the conditions, and a lack of public support? The answer likely lies in the deterrence logic that motivates immigration enforcement and criminal justice policies alike. The Trump administration probably believes that word will spread about the inhumane conditions, and this will in turn diminish the desire of at least some migrants to come to the United States. Scholars of migration have long pointed out, however, that these deterrence logics suffer from the same fatal flaw: they cannot stop the drive to migrate, nor have punitive immigration policies been shown to deter migrants (Cornelius 2005; De Leon 2015; Valdez 2016; Ryo 2019). Inhumane conditions in detention inflict trauma and harm onto children and their families without actually serving any tangible policy benefit beyond dehumanizing migrants. Cynically, one may suggest this might be the intended goal of such policies.

3.11 Public Support for Family Separation

Given public outcry over family separation and widespread calls to end the practice, we sought to measure what, if any, public support there is for the policy. We wanted to determine if the same factors that drive border wall support, such as partisanship, cultural and demographic threat, and racial attitudes, also explain support for family separation. The overall results indicate that there is strong disapproval of the policy, with 60 percent expressing strong opposition and another 20 percent indicating that they "somewhat oppose" it. Significant differences by party remain. Democrats overwhelmingly reject family separation, with 97 percent expressing some level of opposition (85 percent strongly and 12 percent somewhat opposed). Republicans are split on this policy, with about half expressing support and half expressing opposition. Approval for family separation among Republicans is weak, however, as only 17 percent strongly support separation. While there are discernable partisan differences in support of child detention and family separation, it is noteworthy that Republicans are far less supportive of these policies than they are of the border wall.

Considering the role of cultural threat in driving attitudes toward family separation, we also observe significant differences in opinion. Among people who express low levels of cultural threat, 74 percent strongly oppose the policy, and another 16 percent somewhat oppose it. This totals to 90 percent opposition. Those with high levels of cultural threat, by contrast, express a total of 49 percent opposition, with a much greater amount expressing somewhat oppose (31 percent) than strongly oppose (18 percent). This represents a difference in both the degree of opposition and a 41-point difference in total opposition between those who express low and high levels of threat. Only 2 percent of low-threat people express strong support for the policy, compared to 19 percent of high-threat individuals. While there are marked differences in support between these groups, it is worth noting that even among the high-threat group, there is significant ambiguity in their opinions, with a third of high-threat respondents indicating "somewhat support" (32 percent) or "somewhat oppose" (31 percent). Attitudes toward family separation are far less solidified and polarized than are attitudes toward the border wall. However, they are not as uniform in opposition as are opinions of child detention.

Turning to our statistical models, we find that several key factors drive support for family separation (see Figure 4). Consistent with our theoretical expectations and prior results, we see that being a Republican is associated with a 12 percentage-point increase in support for family separation. This result is

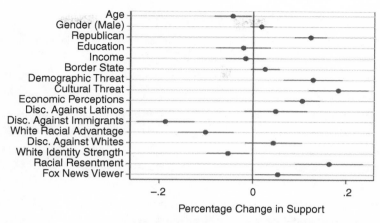

Note: Coefficient plot (OLS) indicating percentage point change in support for the relevant outcome. Lines indicate 95 percent confidence intervals.

Figure 4 Support for family separation

not surprising, given that the policy was implemented by a Republican president and overall support for it is higher among Republicans. Both cultural and demographic threat also have a sizeable impact on support, associated with an 18 percentage-point and nearly 13 percentage-point increase, respectively, for those who express higher levels of threat. Further, people who are more racially resentful are also more likely to support family separation (a 16 percentage-point change). If people are worried, feel threatened by immigration, and hold negative racial attitudes, it is not a large theoretical jump to believe that they are more likely to support a punitive immigration policy that is largely directed at Latinos. Finally, those most negative in their economic perceptions of the country are also more likely to support this policy (a 10 percentage-point change).

Similar to wall opinion, we find evidence that a few factors appreciably reduce support for family separation. Those who hold racially progressive attitudes, such as acknowledging white privilege and recognizing the discrimination that immigrants face, are much less likely to support family separation. In particular, perceptions of discrimination toward immigrants results in a nearly 19 percentage-point decrease in support. We believe these results are consistent with the idea that people who hold racially progressive attitudes are more likely to be able to anticipate the negative consequences of these types of policies, as well as who will be most negatively impacted. Overall, our results provide robust evidence that partisanship, threat, and racial attitudes do play a vital role in explaining support for and opposition to family separation.

3.12 Conclusion

Trump's "zero-tolerance" family separation and child caging practices are arguably his most controversial immigration policies to date. Yet, as the data presented in this section indicate, the country seems to be strongly against these policies, particularly child detention. Furthermore, in sharp contrast to the administration's attempts to end the Flores Agreement, white Americans – including Republicans – overwhelmingly believe that migrant minors who are taken into custody should not be denied basic rights and necessities. Thus, despite the rabid nativism of Trump's rhetoric and actions, we seem to have found a moral threshold in the types of punitive immigration policies that components of his base are willing to support. Nevertheless, as we've also shown, racial attitudes continue to shape the thinking of those who do back the president's most penal immigration practices.

Given Trump's bigoted anti-Latino rhetoric, it is not surprising that our statistical results revealed that respondents who believe Latino immigrants are a cultural threat to the country, who are more racially resentful, and who are anxious about the nation's growing racial diversity are also much more likely to support family separation. Thus, the fact that the president continues to push for punishing immigration policies despite large-scale public opposition to them suggests that he is playing to a particular segment of his party: the most racially prejudiced.

Whether supportive attitudes toward Trump's most punitive immigration policies are amenable to change when people learn about their negative consequences is the question we take up next.

4 Can Information Shift Policy Opinions?

Don't believe the crap you see from these people, the fake news … What you're seeing and what you're reading is not what's happening.

– President Donald Trump, 2018

In the current political environment, questions frequently swirl about the accuracy of statements made by the president, political elites, in media reports, or in campaign ads.[14] Many scholars and pundits have focused on how "fake news" or disinformation can shape public opinion and the polity more generally (Lazer et al. 2018). There is also increasing attention paid to whether people are able to distinguish facts from opinions in a politically polarized era (Dimock 2019). Recent polling data by the Pew Research Center indicate that over 50 percent of people believe that "made-up news and information" is a very big problem in the country today (Mitchell et al. 2019). This information environment poses unique challenges for immigration politics, because the issue has historically been plagued by low levels of political information among the public and elites, as well as considerable misinformation and promulgation of stereotypes about immigrants and immigration (Chavez 2001; Haynes et al. 2016).

In this section, we focus on information and its role in shaping attitudes on immigration policy. Dire consequences and serious harms result from policies such as child detention and border fortification. It is unclear if members of the public are aware of these costs and, if so, how this might impact their support of the policies that generate them. For this reason, we designed a survey experiment on each of the policies we study – the border wall, child detention, and family separation – to assess whether information about their negative consequences decreases support for them.

4.1 Information and Public Opinion

One of the fundamental principles underlying a representative democracy is the idea that the public has some level of political knowledge. But most people possess low levels of political knowledge (Delli Carpini & Skeeter 1996), which raises a number of concerns about how public beliefs shape policy preferences (Gilens 2001). Kuklinski et al. (2000) contend that misinformation, where people hold strong beliefs that are factually incorrect, is particularly troubling. They suggest the problem is less that people hold wrong beliefs but rather that they feel very confident their beliefs are right. Misinformation can operate to strongly shape opinions and political behavior. Nyhan (2010), for example, shows that the "death panel" myth that was part of the debate on the

---

[14] Epigraph from Cillizza (2018).

Affordable Care Act is a prime example of misinformation: not only was it false, but it strongly motivated people to oppose the legislation. People can also engage in motivated reasoning, where they process information only insofar as it conforms with their preexisting beliefs, rejecting new information that is incongruent with those beliefs (Redlawsk 2002; Flynn et al. 2017). Motivated reasoning creates extreme resistance to changing opinions in response to new information that conflicts with prior beliefs; inconsistent information may even produce backfire effects, causing people to dig their heels in on their incorrect prior beliefs (Taber & Lodge 2006; Nyhan & Reifler 2010).

Research continually confirms that it is tremendously difficult to effectively correct misinformation (Nyhan et al. 2013; Nyhan & Reifler 2015). Nyhan (2010) suggests that rather than trying to correct information, it may be more useful to increase the reputational costs to dishonest political elites of spreading false information. Another alternative may be providing factual information on a topic in a way that is not specifically designed to correct false beliefs. Jerit and Zhao (2020) note that research is mixed on how to best correct misinformation, and they suggest it will be much more difficult to do so on hot-button issues. Immigration likely represents a hard case to test whether correct information can change beliefs. Rather than specifically correcting misinformation, our experiments are designed to provide factual information about a policy with a focus on the potential negative consequences involved. Past research in other salient issue areas, such as the war in Iraq (Berinsky 2009) and health care and welfare (Kuklinski et al. 2000), has shown that providing factual information about the issues, including costs and harms, did not shift opinion on them. This suggests that information may not be that effective in moving opinion on immigration.

Scholarship indicates that immigration is not different from other issue areas in terms of the low levels of political knowledge and misperceptions (Citrin & Sides 2008). The use of stereotypes about immigrants and immigration in media and political elite discourse is pervasive (Chavez 2001; Jones-Correa & de Graauw 2013). Additionally, people who are more anxious about immigration demonstrate patterns of bias in information processing because they are more likely to read, remember, and seek out threatening information on immigration (Gadarian & Albertson 2014). Opinion on immigration is also highly sensitive to how the issue is framed (Haynes et al. 2016; Wallace & Wallace 2020). Testing whether information can correct attitudes on immigration, Hopkins et al. (2019) show that providing correct information about the actual size of the immigrant population, for example, does not have much effect on people's beliefs about the size of the population or their immigration attitudes more broadly.

In this section, we contribute to this literature by testing whether information about the impact of Trump's immigration policies can shift support.

4.2 Analytical Advantages of Experiments

Social scientists often utilize experiments in various settings, such as laboratories, the field, or surveys, to assess the impact of information (Druckman et al. 2011). One advantage to doing so is that it makes it possible to advance causal claims about whether the information provided in the experiment (the treatments) can actually shift public opinion relative to the control. When designing experiments, it is critical to be cognizant of the need for external validity (Campbell & Stanley 1966; Calder et al. 1982). External validity "refers to the generalizability of the findings of a study or the extent to which conclusions can be applied across different populations or situations" (McDermott, 2011: 34). McDermott (2011) notes that political scientists are particularly concerned about the artificiality or triviality of experimental designs compared to real-life conditions. We ground the design of our experiments in media and expert accounts of the impact of immigration policies in order to ensure that they reflect actual and likely real-world impacts.

Experiments can offer vital analytical leverage in examining the conditions under which we can shift opinions on immigration. More broadly, it is also important to determine whether information matters in today's era of polarization and in the presence of so much disinformation and misinformation. Because immigration is currently understood to be one of the most polarizing issues, it is possible that no information is able to overcome cognitive dissonance and motivated reasoning on this issue. Indeed, we may expect that providing accurate information on this issue may actually make people dig into their prior positions, as has been shown in other issue areas such as Obamacare and vaccines (Nyhan et al. 2013). If we are able to shift immigration attitudes with accurate information about the negative consequences of particular policies, this may provide us some space for optimism, both in terms of correcting a lack of information or misinformation and in terms of the possibilities for immigration reform and agreement on immigration policies.

4.3 The Catastrophic Costs of Trump's Policies

Serious human, fiscal, economic, and environmental costs have often resulted from immigration enforcement measures, all of which the current president's policies only magnify. For example, the most devastating effect of Trump's wall would undoubtedly be an increase in the number of migrant deaths along the US–Mexico partition. As previously discussed, border bulwarks first accelerated in the mid-1990s, part of a strategy called "prevention through deterrence" (PTD) (De Leon, 2015: 23). PTD's goal was to thwart undocumented immigration by literally putting the lives of crossing migrants in "mortal danger": the policy established border fortifications designed to "funnel" them away from urban areas and into "rugged mountains and brutal deserts" (Herweck & Nicol 2018: 13). The human costs of this policy have been disastrous. The annual number of known migrant deaths near the border jumped from 171 in 1994, the year PTD was announced, to an average of 460 during Trump's first three years in office (Rosenblum 2012: 33; International Organization for Migration 2020). The most recent Border Patrol figures show that from 1998 through 2019, over 7,800 dead migrant bodies were discovered along our southwestern national boundary, an average of about 355 a year (US Border Patrol 2019). The agency notoriously undercounts these casualties, however, and fails to include remains found by local authorities and NGOs (GAO 2006; Ortega 2018). Although it is impossible to get an accurate calculation, scholars and investigative reports estimate that the number of migrant deaths may actually be 300 percent higher than the Border Patrol contends (Weber & Pickering 2011: 1; O'Dell, Gonzalez, & Castellano 2017). That is, the figure is possibly over 23,400, and it will only increase if the president's goal of doubling the miles of existing border bulwarks materializes.

Earlier we reviewed various policies that gave presidential administrations the power to waive laws – including environmental ones – to build walls. These actions have resulted in border fortifications causing serious damage to hundreds of acres of some of the most biologically diverse regions and sensitive ecosystems on the continent (Cohn 2007; Peters et al. 2018). More walls at the border would be fatal to numerous endangered plant and animal species, including various types of insects, fish, birds, and mammals, which have already begun to perish at higher rates due to the erection of existing border barriers, stadium lighting, and patrolling (Eriksson & Taylor 2008). Furthermore, current fortifications have ruined vital waterways and natural drainage systems, inadvertently creating makeshift dams that capture debris and cause massive flooding that results in portions of border fences sinking into the ground (Sierra Club 2015; Herweck & Nicol 2018: 23–36). More walling would certainly lead to more environmental destruction, much of which may be irreversible.

Trump's proposal to build a border wall would additionally come at a high financial cost to taxpayers. While the president and the DHS claim that a fortification along the nearly 2,000-mile US–Mexico divide would "only" cost between $15 and 22 billion, the conservative Cato Institute and a Senate Democrat Report put the price tag closer to $59.8 to 70 billion, not including overrun and maintenance fees, none of which "Mexico would pay for," as Trump repeatedly promised (Felbab-Brown 2017; Nowrasteh 2019). These estimates are important to highlight, given that since the mid-1990s the disdain of many Americans "for a government that is unable to balance its books" has permeated the politics of immigration (Calavita 1996: 295). Thus, whether they agree with the policy or not, citizens who are adamant about eliminating, lowering, or, at the very least, not increasing the national debt may find the true projected cost of the president's wall concerning.

Regardless of the Constitution's protection of private property and the initial constrains of eminent domain, hundreds of home and landowners "have already been forced to give up their property," often at below market value (Herweck & Nicol 2018: 4, 37–38). Assessments suggest that Trump's border wall could affect up to five thousand additional property owners, leading to legal battles that may drag on for decades and cost taxpayers millions (Trapasso 2019). Unsurprisingly, race seems to play a role in whose land gets taken and whose is spared. Properties with more Latino, Native-American, poor, less educated, and foreign-born residents have historically been more likely to be confiscated by federal authorities to build border fortifications (Wilson et al. 2008). As Gilman (2011) adds, numerous small landowners have already "lost their property to the wall while more lucrative developed properties and resorts were not included" in its path, despite being similarly situated on the borderline (276). Thus, existing US border walls are not only metaphorically and historically white supremacist, they are also geographically and demographically racist. Given that Trump is a real estate mogul who has previously been sued by the Justice Department for racially discriminatory practices, there is no reason for us to believe that his wall-building behavior will be any different when it comes to which border residents have their properties seized (Lopez 2019).

According to the Office of the Inspector General, the separation of families in detention has been historically "rare," occurring "because of circumstances such as the parent's medical emergency or a determination that the parent was a threat to the child's safety" (OIG, 2019: 3). The rarity of these actions is debatable (see Section 3 and ARC 2011), but, as is now well known, President Trump's "zero-tolerance" family separation policy officially sanctioned, enacted, and exposed the large-scale practice of forcibly ripping migrant child detainees away from their mothers and fathers. While the exact number of family separations is undetermined, we know it is in the thousands (Holpuch 2019). Personal accounts by detainees reveal that children were taken from their parents without being told where they were going, sometimes under the pretext of being bathed, and never returned (Domonoske & Gonzalez 2018). Toddlers and babies only a few months old have been stripped from their mothers and fathers without knowing when or if they would be reunited, with some children being separated from their parents for up to eight months (Washington Post 2018). According to the former head of ICE, many of these kids will likely never see their parents again (Joyce 2018). This is because, in addition to federal authorities "losing" over a thousand of these minors (Montini 2019), many migrant kids are being "handed over" to powerful and wealthy conservative Christian families who are able to petition for legal custody of them (Filipovic 2019).

Equally reprehensible are Border Patrol agents allegedly "weaponizing" the threat of putting migrant kids up for adoption as a way to discipline child detainees and pressure parents to give up their asylum claims (Joyce 2018). According to the American Academy of Pediatrics 2018, this type of family separation can cause "irreparable harm to children." As a Harvard Medical School professor explained, "the abrupt separation of children from their parents is a huge psychological trauma and assault," the magnitude of which "cannot be overstated." Prolonged separation from their parents, isolation, and placement in institutional settings can be potentially "life-threatening," he explains: "It disrupts the brain circuits, it disrupts the immune system, it disrupts metabolic systems, and it sets the stage for lifelong problems with physical health and mental health" (Chotiner 2019).

The framing of "family separation as slow death" is understandable upon learning about the conditions of separated children's confinement, leading one pediatrician to describe the detention center they toured as akin to "torture facilities" (Lee 2019; NPR 2019). Some migrants have been held in outdoor "tent cities" or fenced in under bridges, forced to sleep on the ground. Indoor detention is not much better, with up to 900 people being held cramped in facilities designed to hold only 125 (Lind 2019). Children are often "locked in their cells and cages nearly all day long" (Smith 2019), which are frequently set to freezing temperatures, where they are forced to sleep on the floor with bright lights shining on their faces all night (Chapin 2019). Migrant minors have reported being bullied and verbally and physically abused by guards (Silva 2018), who take their blankets and sleeping mats away as punishment (Stieb 2019). Not only have numerous minors and adults died while in ICE custody – including twenty-six in the first two years of the Trump administration (Sawyer 2019) – but migrant children have also reported being forcibly drugged with "psychotropic medications" (Bogado 2018) and thousands have described being sexually abused while in detention (Davila-Ruhaak et al., 2014: 4–7; Ryo, 2019: 104; and Gonzales 2019).

Physical abuse also manifests in the form of neglect. Children under the age of three have been left alone screaming with no one to take care of them, without clean clothes, toothbrushes, or medical attention, despite being "feverish, coughing, vomiting" and with diarrhea (Long 2019: 3–4; Chapin 2019). Migrant kids are often left in conditions described as chaotic scenes of "sickness and filth" (Dickerson 2019), without basic sanitation, and are denied showers and adequate food or water, which when sick is "tantamount to intentionally causing the spread of disease" (Stieb 2019). Under Trump, ICE and Border Patrol agents seem to be taking their cruelty to new heights, openly laughing at crying migrant toddlers in cages via text and, in Facebook groups, joking about dead Latino babies and calling migrants "beaners" (Thompson 2019) and "disgusting subhuman shit unworthy of being kindling for a fire" (Echavarri 2019). The actual and predicted harms and disastrous consequences of Trump's immigration policies lay bare the dire stakes of supporting and enacting his agenda.

4.4 General Analytical Approach

In each of our experiments, we utilize a similar design focused on the negative consequences of a given policy and its effect on opinion. We provide all survey respondents with a small amount of background so that everyone has some baseline information before they answer our questions about their level of support for or opposition to that policy. The source of the information provided is experts. Although Jerit and Zhao (2020) note that in polarized times people may be more skeptical of expert sources, we believe that information coming from experts is more likely be viewed as neutral, less partisan, and legitimate. We also wanted the treatment to be credible, and using a neutral source like experts seemed significantly more plausible than drawing material sourced from political elites of each party. Historically, elites have also employed scientific expert testimony to get immigration legislation passed (Tichenor 2002), and knowledge from experts on immigration can lend authority to positions (Boswell 2009). Even in an era when the public expresses skepticism about facts and the reliability of sources of information, there is evidence that the public still trusts experts to weigh in on policy (Funk et al. 2019).

In each experiment, individuals are randomly assigned to a group; the groups are roughly equal in size. Respondents read either only the paragraph of background information (control group) or read an additional passage focused on a negative consequence (treatment group). Overall, we expect partisanship, cultural and demographic threat, and racial attitudes will significantly affect whether any of the information provided in the survey experiments shifts attitudes. Given the high levels of opposition to these policies among Democrats, we expect that none of the treatments will do much to decrease their support, because there is little room to reduce it further. Among Republicans, on the other hand, we expect that in certain circumstances we will observe some movement in opinion. Given the strong role of cultural threat in driving support for these immigration policies, we also expect threat to condition whether information decreases support of these policies. In what follows, we discuss the design of each experiment, our theoretical expectations, and our results.

4.5 Wall Experiment Design

Our wall experiment focuses on the human, fiscal, environmental, and property costs of building the border wall. We focused on these dimensions because we believed they were the most likely to shift opinions. Given extremely high levels of support on this specific issue from Republicans and those with high levels of cultural threat, however, it may be difficult to reduce support for the wall through providing this information.

All survey respondents read the following text:

> The border patrol uses many enforcement strategies along the US–Mexico border, including patrol cars and planes, various types of physical barriers, and technological surveillance such as drones, high-powered lights, and motion sensors. Recent proposals include constructing a wall across nearly the entire almost 2,000-mile-long US–Mexico border.

Our first treatment is concerned with increased migrant deaths. Despite fervent support among some segments of the population, particularly Republicans and those who feel culturally threatened, we expect providing information about deaths could trigger a moral limit in respondents, whereby the policy becomes not permissible as a result. The text for this treatment reads:

> Experts have said that the completion of a border wall would result in an increase in the number of undocumented migrants who die attempting to cross the border. (*Death Treatment*)

The second treatment draws attention to private property that would have to be seized by the federal government in order to build the border wall. Any president who wishes to complete a wall along the entire US–Mexico border will have to employ litigation to seize hundreds of acres of private lands via eminent domain. Given the historical investment in property rights (Paul 2017), we expect this cost might reduce support for the wall, particularly among Republicans and conservatives. The text of the treatment is this:

> Experts have said that the completion of a border wall would result in loss of private land by property owners in the US. (*Property Loss Treatment*)

The third treatment centers on fiscal costs. Our treatment does not employ the highest estimates of the cost to build a wall, but rather a moderate estimate. We expect that some individuals may view the economic cost of the wall as too high, even if they generally support the policy. The cost of the wall may decrease Republican or conservative support for the wall the most because these groups are more likely to describe themselves as fiscal conservatives who are worried about increasing the national debt (Skocpol & Williamson 2016). The text of that treatment reads:

Experts have said that the completion of a border wall would increase the national debt with estimated costs of over $20 Billion. (*Cost Treatment*)

Our last treatment in the wall experiment involves environmental impacts. While environmental concerns may only appeal to very liberal respondents, we thought that given extensive public debate on climate change, it might be possible for environmental concerns to shift opinion, though we did not have strong expectations that environmental concerns would decrease support. The text of this treatment is as follows:

Experts have said that the completion of a border wall would result in significant environmental harm to ecosystems, endangered species. (*Environmental Treatment*)

After reading the vignette on the border wall, respondents were asked, "Do you support or oppose construction of the border wall?" They were given answer choices of "Strongly Support," "Somewhat Support," "Somewhat Oppose," and "Strongly Oppose."[15]

4.6 Shifting Support for the Wall

Our results indicate that the effect of information on wall support is quite limited. All Figures containing the results of the experiments display the first differences of the treatments relative to the control on support for the wall, with 95 percent confidence intervals indicated by the lines. Figure 5 displays the overall results and shows that information has no impact on wall support, as none of the treatments shifted opinion in a statistically significant way. Due to the level of polarization in border wall support, however, it may be most fruitful to examine conditional effects by partisanship (see Figure 6).[16] None of the information reduced Democratic support. Levels of support for the border wall across the various treatment groups among Democrats were all in the single digits. Likewise, support for the wall among independents was not affected by information. Among Republicans, only one negative consequence influenced support for the wall: information about the fiscal cost of the wall reduced Republican support by 11 percentage points, with 85 percent support among people in the control group compared to 74 percent among those who

---

[15] The placement of the survey experiments on this survey (ITES) was after the observational questions about the wall, child detention, and family separation. We did this to avoid contamination from the treatments in the experiments and to be able to assess the entire sample's viewpoints on the policies independently.

[16] We also examined ideological differences by comparing liberals to moderates to conservatives. The results are the same in effects and magnitude, with only the cost of the wall reducing conservatives' support of the wall by 12 percentage points. The results are in Appendix B.

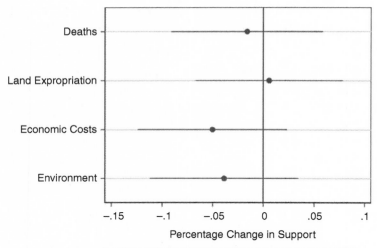

Note: Percentage point change compared to the control group in support
for the relevant outcome. Lines indicate 95 percent confidence intervals.

Figure 5 Wall experiment overall treatment effects

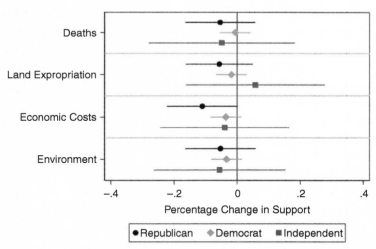

Note: Percentage point change compared to the control group in support
for the relevant outcome. Lines indicate 95 percent confidence intervals.

Figure 6 Wall experiment treatment effects, conditional on partisanship

received the economic costs treatment. Still, this group of respondents
strongly supports the wall overall. The effects of learning about the cost of
wall are not substantial enough to drive Republican support below the 50 percent threshold.

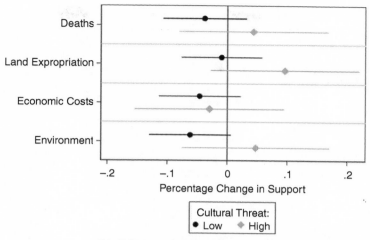

Figure 7 Wall experiment treatment effects, conditional on cultural threat

In Figure 7, we compare the effects of the treatments among people who express high and low levels of cultural threat. There are significant differences in raw levels of support, with people with high levels of cultural threat expressing 76 percent support for the wall, compared to only 17 percent support among those with low levels of cultural threat. Despite this raw difference in support, the information in the treatments about the costs of the wall did not reduce support for the policy in either group. Our results confirm that it may be difficult to use information to change opinion on deeply polarized issues. From a normative perspective, the inability of information about severe consequences of the wall – such as increased death of migrants – to reduce support is especially concerning.

4.7 Child Detention Experiment Design

In Section 3, our results showed that the vast majority of survey respondents chose the least restrictive policy option regarding the detention of migrant children, which was to release children to sponsors or family. Only a very small percentage of people selected putting children in detention facilities as the best policy option. Here we focus on whether people agree or disagree that migrant children should be held in immigrant detention facilities. The design of our survey experiment on child detention is centered on the poor conditions of detention, including abuse. We focused on the most egregious forms of abuse that we thought were the most likely to shift opinion. The treatments provide information on reported sexual abuse, death, physical abuse, being locked in cages for long periods of time, and denying children adequate food and water while they are in detention facilities. Of course, other forms of abuse, such as verbal and psychological abuse where guards taunt children about deporting them or separating them from their parents, are also quite harmful to children. But given that our goal was to see if we could move opinion, we expected that physical forms of abuse might provoke an even stronger reduction in support for child detention.

By focusing on abuse and poor conditions, we hope that some respondents will be triggered by the failure of the government to protect children in their custody. We believe that information on the abuses may cross a moral threshold, whereby it delegitimizes the policy and causes proponents to weigh whether child detention is worth these costs. Even among groups who may support this policy or think it permissible in the abstract, such as Republicans or those with high levels of cultural threat, it is possible that views will shift when participants learn about the grave abuses and appalling conditions of child detention.

All respondents read the following background paragraph to provide some general information about children in detention:

> An increasing number of migrant children, who are under 18, are being held in immigrant detention facilities by federal immigration authorities. Some of these children entered the U.S. as unaccompanied minors and others were separated from their parents by immigration authorities.

The first treatment focuses on sexual abuse that has occurred while children are in custody. Abuse, whether sexual or physical, implies that government employees in detention centers are not only engaging in the abuse but also failing to adequately supervise and monitor the children in order to prevent abuse from occurring. We expect that if opinions are going to move as a result of information, the gravity of sexual abuse could result in that effect.

> While in these facilities, children have been sexually assaulted. (*Sexual Abuse Treatment*)

The second treatment provides information about children being held in locked rooms or cages. The information indicates that children are being held in prison-like conditions with extremely limited movement over a twenty-four-hour period. This type of restricted movement is similar to solitary confinement, which involves a minimum of twenty-two hours per day of confinement in a cell (Guenther 2013). With regard to juvenile criminal detention facilities, solitary confinement is extremely irregular, and there have been growing calls to end the practice (Lee 2016; Clark 2017). The text of this treatment is as follows:

> While in these facilities, children have been held in locked rooms or cages for nearly 24 hours a day. (*Cages Treatment*)

The third treatment is also on the conditions of detention. Recall from Section 3 that our results show respondents were highly supportive of children having access to appropriate amounts of food and water while in detention (with over 88 percent agreement). Given the overwhelming public support for adequate food and water, we expect that information about depriving immigrant children of food and water may reduce support for child detention. The text of the treatment is this:

> While in these facilities, children have had limited access to food and water. (*Food and Water Treatment*)

The fourth treatment addresses the deaths of children in detention. While rare, there has been a marked increase in migrant deaths in detention during the Trump presidency, including those of child migrants. These deaths occurred when children were sick while in custody and failed to receive adequate and timely emergency health care despite their greater vulnerability to illness and complications (Acevedo 2019). We expect that some people may be less supportive of detention if they are aware of these deaths, given the gravity and permanence of death. The text of this treatment reads:

> While in these facilities, children have died in custody. (*Death Treatment*)

The final treatment concerns physical abuse of migrant children. We expect that this information could shift opinion because of the physical nature of the abuse and harm involved. Learning about children being beaten could trigger a sense of moral outrage about their being subjected to physical harm at the hands of guards. The text of the treatment is as follows:

> While in these facilities, children have been physically beaten. (*Physical Abuse Treatment*)

After the participants read the vignette on child detention, we asked all respondents, "Do you agree or disagree that the federal government should hold migrant children in detention facilities?" The answer choices were "Strongly Agree," "Somewhat Agree," "Somewhat Disagree," and "Strongly Disagree."

4.8 Shifting Support for Detention

Our results reported in Section 3 confirm that support for child detention is low. Only 7 percent of respondents indicated they strongly agreed that children should be detained, with another 14 percent indicating they somewhat agreed, for a total of 21 percent support and 79 percent opposition. Stronger raw support for the policy is expressed by Republicans and people who feel high levels of

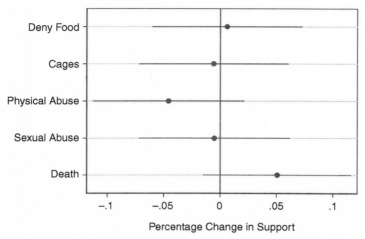

Note: Percentage point change compared to the control group in support
for the relevant outcome. Lines indicate 95 percent confidence intervals.

Figure 8 Child detention experiment overall treatment effects

cultural threat. Among Republicans, 20 percent strongly agree and another 34 percent somewhat agree with child detention. Likewise, among people who feel the highest levels of cultural threat, 22 percent strongly support the policy, and nearly 32 percent somewhat support it. Our results in Section 3 indicated, however, that faced with a broader question about what to do when children are in the custody of immigration authorities, all groups of respondents, including Republicans and those with high levels of cultural threat, expressed the strongest support for the least restrictive option of releasing children to families or sponsors.

Turning to whether the information provided in the experiment affects support for child detention relative to the control, we find no statistically significant effects of the treatments in the overall sample (see Figure 8). We also do not observe any statistically significant effects among specific subsamples who express higher support for the policy, such as Republicans (see Figure 9) or those with high levels of cultural threat (see Figure 10).[17] These results confirm that providing accurate information about the harms of child detention policy does not move opinion. These findings are consistent with prior work that demonstrates it can be quite difficult to move opinions by providing factual information, particularly on highly salient issues. Normatively, the implications are incredibly important, because information about the extremely

---

[17] We also do not observe any treatment effects in reducing support among conservatives relative to the control. The results are in Appendix B.

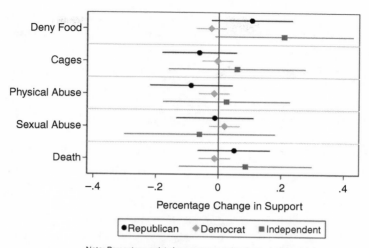

Figure 9 Child detention experiment treatment effects, conditional on partisanship

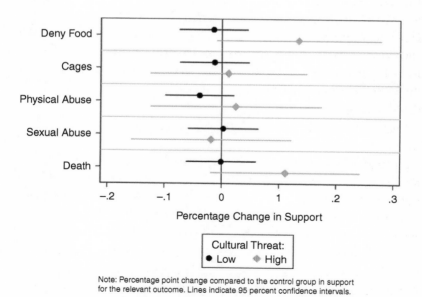

Figure 10 Child detention experiment treatment effects, conditional on cultural threat

poor conditions in detention and the grave abuses inflicted on migrant children failed to reduce support for the policy. The willingness to allow a policy even when informed about the grave human harms that result from it confirms that opinions on this issue are fairly fixed among those who support it, and that no kind of information may ever be able to reduce their approval.

4.9 Family Separation Experiment Design

While there has been considerable media attention around family separation, it is unclear if the public has much knowledge of the long-term effects or the conditions experienced by immigrants as a result of the policy. Our experiment focuses on the fact that family separation can occur for long periods of time, result in psychological harm and in children not knowing when they will see their parents again, and even result in some migrant children being put up for adoption without parental consent. Our goal is to identify if knowledge of the negative consequences of the policy can shift people to oppose the policy. All respondents read the following background information:

> When federal immigration authorities have migrant families in their custody, they often separate them by sending adults and children to different detention facilities.

The first treatment highlights that separations can occur for a long time. It is possible that people who support the policy may believe separation is usually quite brief. If people become aware that separations can result in children being held apart from their families for a substantial amount of time, they may be less supportive. The text of the treatment reads as follows:

> When this separation occurs, experts have found that it can result in families separated for very long periods of time. (*Long Time Separated Treatment*)

The second treatment centers on the psychological effects of family separation. In this sense, this treatment is focused on a negative consequence that results from the policy. Individuals may not realize that family separation can cause long-term psychological harm, such as separation anxiety, permanent bonding problems with their family, and post-traumatic stress disorder (Newman & Steel 2008; Suárez Orozco et al. 2011). The text of the treatment reads:

> When this separation occurs, experts have found that it can result in psycho-logical damage. (*Psychological Treatment*)

The third treatment concerns the uncertainty children face from the process of separation. It is very traumatic and unsettling for children to not know when they will be reunited with their parents. If this type of emotional stress to children may cross a moral threshold that makes the policy unacceptable, then we may observe a decline in support. The text of the third treatment is as follows:

> When this separation occurs, experts have found that it can result in children not knowing when they will be able to see their parents again. (*Not Knowing Treatment*)

The final treatment focuses on migrant children who are put up for adoption without parental consent. There have been cases where immigration authorities placed children who were unaccompanied or who were separated from their parents in foster care, and some judges allowed adoptions to occur (Rodrigo 2018). Immigration authorities have also placed some migrant children in the care of one of the largest adoption agencies, which heightened concern that the children would be put up for adoption (Joyce 2018). While this occurrence has been rare, we wanted to test whether this consequence, which permanently separates parents from children, would reduce support for family separation. The text of the treatment is as follows:

> When this separation occurs, experts have found that it can result in migrant children being put up for adoption without parental consent. (*Adoption Treatment*)

After reading the vignette on family separation, all respondents were asked, "Do you support or oppose separating immigrant families being held by federal immigration authorities?" They could select answer choices ranging from "Strongly Support" to "Strongly Oppose."

4.10 Shifting Support for Family Separation

Recall from Section 3 that we found support for family separation significantly more likely among Republicans and those who feel high levels of demographic and cultural threat. Here, we shift our attention to analyze how providing information about the negative impacts of family separation influences support for the policy. Relative to the control, our overall results indicate that information did not move opinion (see Figure 11). We also examine whether there are conditional effects among those most likely to support the policy (i.e., Republicans and those with high levels of cultural threat) in order to see if information can reduce their support. Similar to the experiment on child detention, we do not find any statistically significant effects for any of the treatments among these groups (see Figures 12 and 13).[18] It is quite disconcerting to learn

---

[18] We do not find any treatment effects in moving conservative support for the policy. The results are in Appendix B.

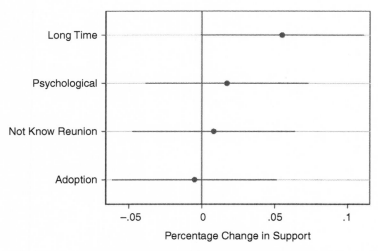

Note: Percentage point change compared to the control group in support
for the relevant outcome. Lines indicate 95 percent confidence intervals.

Figure 11 Family separation experiment overall treatment effects

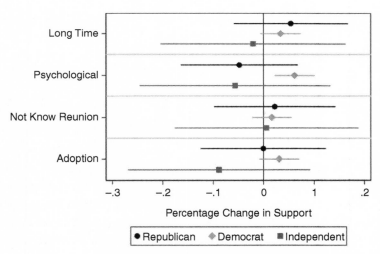

Note: Percentage point change compared to the control group in support
for the relevant outcome. Lines indicate 95 percent confidence intervals.

Figure 12 Family separation experiment treatment effects, conditional on
partisanship

that informing respondents about negative consequences such as psychological
harm or the adoption of migrant children without parental consent does not
reduce levels of support for family separation. If supporters' opinions are

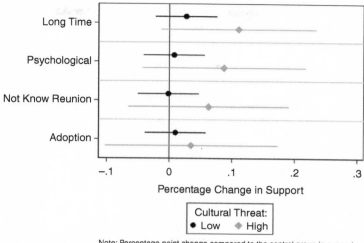

Note: Percentage point change compared to the control group in support for the relevant outcome. Lines indicate 95 percent confidence intervals.

Figure 13 Family separation experiment treatment effects, conditional on cultural threat

cemented to this degree, it is unclear whether any type of information is capable of shifting their views.

4.11 Stereotypes and Immigration

While our survey experiments focus on the nexus of information shifting support for immigration policies, it is also useful to assess how much misinformation there is about immigration. One type of misinformation is belief in false stereotypes about immigrants. Immigration as a policy issue has long been mired in misinformation and stereotypes (Chavez 2008; Haynes et al. 2016). As discussed in previous sections, throughout his presidency Trump has frequently utilized stereotypes and misinformation about immigration and immigrants in an attempt to build support for his policies (Leonhardt & Philbrick 2018). Here, we turn to exploring the pervasiveness of stereotypes of immigrants among the public.

Two of the most common stereotypes about immigrants are related to crime and welfare usage (Chavez 2001; Reny & Manzano 2016). The first stereotype is that immigrants are more likely to commit crimes than native-born US citizens. Many empirical studies conducted by researchers, including liberal and conservative think tanks, have shown this stereotype to be false. Research has demonstrated that immigrants have a *lower* crime rate than natives (Lee 2015; Light & Miller 2018; Flagg 2019). Despite this empirical reality, belief in the stereotype is persistent, and political elites have repeated it ad nauseam.

We asked people to compare how likely they thought it was for undocumented immigrants to commit crimes relative to American citizens. The answer choices were "More Likely," "About as Likely," and "Less Likely." Our data shows nearly 29 percent of respondents believed undocumented immigrants were more likely to commit crimes than American citizens. Fifty-two percent answered "About as Likely," and only 19 percent indicated "Less Likely." Among 2016 Trump voters and Republicans, belief in this stereotype was considerably higher, with nearly 49 percent and 45 percent belief, respectively, compared to only 4 percent of Democrats. Among those who feel high levels of cultural threat, 49 percent expressed the belief that undocumented immigrants were more likely to commit crimes. Given that the most accurate answer was "Less Likely," it is alarming that at least a third of the sample overestimated the propensity of immigrants to engage in crime, and nearly 50 percent of past Trump voters and Republicans did so.

Another dominant stereotype is that immigrants, particularly undocumented immigrants, represent a fiscal burden on the government by using a disproportionate amount of welfare benefits. Since federal welfare reform in 1996, undocumented immigrants have been ineligible for means-tested welfare benefits, and permanent residents are required to wait five years to become eligible (Espenshade et al. 1997). Researchers and think tanks, including conservative think tanks such as the Cato Institute, have found that immigrants use welfare benefits at rates *lower* than US-born citizens (Norwaseth & Orr 2018).

We asked people whether they agreed or disagreed that immigrants today are a burden on the country because they use too many social services, such as welfare. Respondents had four answer choices ranging from "Strongly Agree" to "Strongly Disagree." Overall, 37 percent of respondents agreed that immigrants are a burden (16 percent strongly agree, and 21 percent somewhat agree). A very polarized picture emerges, with much higher levels of agreement expressed by Republican respondents (42 percent strongly agree, and 32 percent somewhat agree), past Trump voters (49 percent strongly agree, and 31 percent somewhat agree), and those who feel high levels of cultural threat (49 percent strongly agree, and 33 percent somewhat agree). In each of these groups, over 74 percent of respondents believe in the false stereotype that immigrants place a burden on social services, compared to only 13 percent of Democrats. These results are distressing, because they confirm that misinformation and beliefs in negative stereotypes about immigrants are widespread and polarized along party lines and lines of cultural threat. Further, this provides some context for why it may have been so difficult to use information as a corrective to immigration attitudes in our experiments.

4.12 Conclusion

This section began by asking whether information about the negative consequences of three of Trump's most controversial immigration policies – the wall, child detention, and family separation – could reduce support for them. Our results overwhelmingly demonstrate that information does little to influence opinion. It does not reduce support, nor does it produce backfire effects that would increase support. The only exception is that information about the cost of the wall has a modest effect on reducing Republican support for that policy. What explains these results? One explanation is that it is very difficult to correct misinformation and use factual information to shift opinions (Nyhan & Reifler 2015; Jerit & Zhao 2020). Our research is consistent with the recent findings of Hopkins et al. (2019), who show that information plays a very limited role in moving attitudes on immigration. Another possibility is that none of the information contained in the treatments is new to the respondents, and thus it is unlikely to shift opinions. This explanation seems weak, however, given low levels of political knowledge and the specificity of some of the information, which was not widely covered in the media. Instead, immigration as an issue may also be too polarizing for information to be effective: given the strength of respondents' prior beliefs about immigration, they may demonstrate cognitive resistance when presented with conflicting information.

Normatively, it is quite concerning that information about the tremendous harms that result from Trump's immigration policies, such as migrant death and abuse in detention facilities, does not decrease support for the border wall or child detention. In light of both the limited role of distressing and disturbing information to move opinion and evidence of widespread belief in dangerous stereotypes, it is hard to imagine conditions under which supporters of Trump's immigration policies could be transformed into opponents. It is even more far-fetched to imagine the conditions under which they would support immigration reform that seeks to expand immigrant rights. If advocates hope to pass immigration reform based on facts about this policy issue, it is particularly troubling to contemplate whether misinformation on immigration can ever be effectively corrected, given the current state of polarized and relatively fixed opinions.

5 Conclusion

Privately, [President Trump] had often talked about fortifying a border wall with a water-filled trench, stocked with snakes or alligators … He wanted the wall electrified, with spikes on top that could pierce human flesh. After publicly suggesting that soldiers should shoot migrants if they threw rocks, the president backed off when his staff told him that was illegal.

– New York Times, 2019

Anthropologist Leo Chavez has long argued that Latinos exist in the American imaginary primarily as dangerous "illegal aliens," "highly fertile invaders," and "unassimilable separatists" (Chavez 2001; Chavez, 2008: 42). In other words, they're perceived to simultaneously pose a criminal, cultural, and demographic threat to a supposedly vulnerable white citizenry that requires, in response, the type of dehumanizing and extreme measures illustrated in the epigraph above.[19] In many respects, the survey data and analyses presented in this Element support the latter assertions, in terms of the factors that help explain the opinions of whites who support Trump's most controversial immigration policies and their reluctance to alter their views when presented with information about the devastating consequences of wall building and immigrant detention.

What is both interesting and troubling about our findings is that despite the fact that the vast majority of Americans disapprove of Trump's draconian immigration practices, racist nativism continues to be the linchpin of his political agenda and reelection bid. This raises the question of why the president would bet his office on such unpopular policies. Our multiple statistical measurements and models indicate that racial attitudes likely help explain Trump's political calculations. Thus, in this final section, we recap some of our principal results and discuss how they help us better comprehend the contemporary politics of immigration.

5.1 White Public Opinion and Trump's Immigration Policies

Our data show that white Americans reject Trump's most punitive actions on immigration. The majority oppose his border wall, for instance, and believe it would be ineffective at blocking undocumented migrants, drugs, or terrorists from entering the country. Only a small proportion of Republicans strongly feel a border wall would be effective in achieving the president's stated aims. Despite the fact that about 80 percent of GOP members strongly support a fortification along our nearly 2,000-mile boundary with Mexico, about half of them do not actually believe it would work. These results imply that Trump's border wall may serve a more figurative than practical function for its supporters.

---

[19] Epigraph from Shear and Hirschfeld Davis (2019).

Our survey respondents even more strongly opposed family separation, including about half of Republicans. The vast majority of our sample said that children in the custody of immigration officials should be released to family members or sponsors. While we anticipated most Democrats would be in favor of this policy option, we did not expect to find that the majority of Republicans would break with the president by indicating that children should be released to relatives or sponsors. In fact, almost no one we polled – including Democrats, Republicans, and independents – expressed support for the idea that minors who are in the custody of immigration officials should be put in detention facilities. We believe that images of screaming babies locked inside chain-link cages were likely too much to stomach, even for those whites who generally hold anti-immigrant views. Consequently, for the first time in his presidency, Trump publicly backed down from a nativist action and signed an executive order to stop family separation – though subsequent reports indicate the practices of child detention and family separation continued (see Section 3).

Most people we surveyed, moreover, think that child detainees should have access to lawyers, psychological services, and language and other educational courses while in custody. Almost everyone expressed support for migrant children receiving appropriate medical care, personal hygiene products, outdoor play time, suitable sleeping accommodations, and adequate amounts of food and water. In other words, while Trump's lawyers have attempted to end the Flores Agreement, which requires many of these basic necessities for kids in detention, whites seem united in their opposition to this aspect of the president's malicious anti-immigrant agenda.

Regardless of public opinion on Trump's border wall, child caging, and family separation policies, our data indicate that he is likely betting his political legacy and the 2020 election on mobilizing the most racially conservative segment of his base through promoting his radically nativist policies. This is important to note because the role of race is seldom considered when exploring the specific factors that drive attitudes about border walls and detention. Yet, as the president has continuously demonstrated, racist tropes about migrants in general – and Latino immigration in particular – serve as his primary justifications for more restrictionist policies. Our findings suggest that the people who back his anti-immigrant platform are also deeply motivated by their negative racial attitudes. We found, for example, that believing Latino immigrants pose a cultural threat to the country, being more racially resentful, and fearing a United States where people of color collectively comprise the majority of the population, all strongly increased the likelihood of supporting Trump's 2,000-mile border wall and of believing it would be effective at stopping "illegal" immigration, terrorism, and drug smuggling. Thus, building on prior work that demonstrates partisanship is key to understanding immigration politics and opinion (Masuoka & Junn, 2013: 9; Abrajano & Hajnal, 2015: 101), our findings show how deeply polarized opinions are on different dimensions of Trump's immigration policy, as well as the vital role that race plays in shaping these beliefs.

Regarding Trump's "zero-tolerance" family separation policy, our results indicate that feeling culturally and demographically threatened, as well as racially resentful, augmented support for this brutal program. While only a small minority of our sample backed the idea of immigration agents putting captured migrant children in detention facilities, the majority of those who expressed high levels of Latino cultural threat supported this devastating action. Alternatively, we also found that whites who acknowledge their racial privilege and believe that immigrants endure high levels of discrimination, are much more likely to be against Trump's wall, kid caging, and family separation practices. Put simply, our data demonstrate that white racial attitudes are key to understanding support for and opposition to the president's anti-immigrant platform.

Given this finding, it is essential to explore whether the white public believes that Trump's policies, which disproportionately impact Latinos, are racist. Accordingly, we asked our survey respondents whether they agreed or disagreed with the following statement: "Donald Trump's actions and rhetoric towards Latino immigrants are racist." Our results revealed stark differences: Among Republicans, nearly 54 percent strongly disagreed, and another 21 percent somewhat disagreed. This adds up to 75 percent of Republicans who reject the notion that the president's behavior on immigration has been racist. Those who voted for Trump in 2016 expressed slightly more disagreement, at nearly 80 percent. In sharp contrast, 83 percent of Democrats strongly agreed, and another nearly 12 percent somewhat agreed, that Trump's immigration policies are racist, for a total of 95 percent. Even if we compare all non-Republicans (Democrats and independents) to Republicans, non-Republicans express 88 percent agreement that Trump's behavior is racist. People who express high levels of cultural threat from Latin American migration also overwhelmingly reject the idea that the president's rhetoric is racist (46 percent strongly disagree, and 23 percent somewhat disagree). These data show the public is deeply divided in how they view and understand the racial implications of the president's conduct.

From a normative standpoint, it is extremely concerning that a large segment of the public views the chief executive's behavior on immigration to be racist toward a specific group, Latino immigrants. These results are not surprising given the extensive record of explicitly racist statements by Trump (Leonhardt & Philbrick 2018; Graham et al. 2019; Lopez 2019). On some level, the prevalence of this behavior with little to no consequence or rebuking of the president must reduce public faith, particularly among people of color, in the leader of the country, its political institutions, and the government more broadly. Potentially more disconcerting is the extent to which Trump's supporters seem unwilling to describe his behavior as what it is, even in the face of objectively racist speech. Either this means that some segments of the public fundamentally misunderstand what it means for something to be racist, or that they are in deep denial about Trump's behavior because acknowledging it would require them to wrestle with how they can still support him despite it, or that they approve of his statements and actions because they also hold the same negative racial viewpoints. None of these explanations bodes well for the health of our democracy or immigration reform in the future.

5.2 Theoretical Implications

If the goals of US border fortification and detention policies are to dissuade undocumented migrants, drug smugglers, and terrorists, as Trump and his presidential predecessors have claimed, then it is critical to point out that billions of wasted dollars and decades of available evidence indicate these practices have not worked. Our harshest immigration enforcement measures can best be understood as what Andreas (2013) calls "politically successful policy failures," in that "they succeeded in terms of their symbolic and image effects even while largely failing in terms of their deterrent effects" (2). As discussed in Sections 2 and 3 of this Element, the symbolisms that walls and cages conjure are those of necessary forms of protection from dangerous migrants seeking to commit violent offenses and steal scant resources from innocent citizens. To quote the president again, "They're beating us economically . . . When Mexico sends its people . . . They're bringing drugs. They're bringing crime. They're rapists" (Mark 2018).

Unfortunately, our data show that the majority of white people – especially those who voted for Trump in 2016 – falsely believe the racist stereotypes that immigrants commit as much or more crime and use more social services than US-born citizens, despite the abundance of research to the contrary. Moreover, as our results on the perceived threat of Latino culture and of a majority-minority nation illustrate, these fears reflect attempts to preserve an imagined white national homogeneity, separating those who are demographically desired from those who are not. This is likely why the president feels comfortable publicly declaring his longing for less immigration from "shithole countries" in Latin America, Africa, and the Caribbean, and more immigration from predominately white nations, such as Norway (Kirby 2018). The demonization and social marginalization that result from this type of rhetoric, in turn, serve as convenient justifications for the exploitation of migrant labor, criminalization of migrants' daily existence, indifference to their abuse, and willful ignorance of the role capitalist Western powers play in contributing to the root causes of global displacements.

Nevertheless, as we explain in the next section, and as President Trump has skillfully shown, symbolically significant policy failures can also be electorally expedient.

5.3 Policy and Electoral Implications

The prospects for passing progressive immigration legislation currently look grim, given how highly polarized both Congress and public opinion are on most aspects of this issue (Abrajano & Hajnal 2015; Wong 2017). This is especially true given that racist attitudes help drive support for anti-immigrant policies, that a substantial segment of the population believes negative and false stereotypes about migrants, and that the public is resistant to changing its opinions when presented with accurate information about the dire consequences of our immigration enforcement practices. That said, our findings also demonstrate that the current administration's child detention and family separation policies are very unpopular and are only weakly supported among the white Republicans who back them. In this sense, the president's policies lack either a public or legal mandate, since Flores does not permit Trump's actions on child detention. While it may be possible for Democrats and Republicans in Congress to agree on some aspects of immigration policy, Trump would likely veto any compromises that could be reached if they did not contain punitive enforcement measures. Hence, the biggest impediment to stopping the building of walls and the caging of migrants is undoubtedly the president himself. Any moderate-to-liberal move on immigration would have to start with the removal of Trump from office. If there is a silver lining in our findings, it is that once this occurs, Republican and Democratic lawmakers need not fear a veto or voter retribution for ending child detention and family separation. A different president would also likely mean less visceral and overtly anti-immigrant rhetoric coming from the nation's chief executive. The likelihood of removing Trump from office, however, will likely depend on how important the issue of immigration is to 2020 election voters and how well they believe Trump has done in handling this policy issue.

We began this Element by discussing how Trump won the 2016 election by mobilizing racially conservative and nativist voters (Jacobson, 2017: 20; Sides et al., 2017: 40; Hooghe & Dassonneville, 2018: 531–532; Schaffner et al., 2018: 10). We have argued that while not all whites back the president's most

brutal border and detention practices, those with the most bigoted racial attitudes tend to. Given the symbolic functions of Trump's most controversial
actions on immigration, we asserted that they are less about reflecting the
country's policy desires than they are about electorally rousing a racially
extreme faction of the public. Indeed, from Charlottesville to Berkeley, we
have continuously seen the president condone the actions of white nationalists
who mobilize in support of him, sometimes with deadly consequences (Sonmez
& Parker 2020). Thus, we believe Trump is likely hinging his legacy and
reelection bid on mobilizing the components of the white electorate who are
anti-immigrant, feel culturally and demographically threatened, and are most
racially resentful.

While we have already shown that people rank immigration as a top issue, we
are also interested in whether it will be a critical factor in which candidate
people decide to vote for. Thus, we asked respondents, "How important will
immigration be to your vote for President in the 2020 election?" Answer choices
included "Not at All Important," "Slightly Important," "Moderately Important,"
"Very Important," and "Extremely Important." Overall, nearly 53 percent
responded that immigration would be extremely or very important to their
vote. Fifty-two percent of Democrats indicated the issue was critical to their
vote choice. Immigration was an even more important factor in vote choice
among Republicans (57 percent) and past Trump voters (64 percent). Likewise,
among those who feel high levels of cultural threat from Latino immigration,
62 percent indicated the issue was very or extremely important to their vote
choice. These results reveal several key insights. First, the overall importance of
immigration remains extremely high across all groups. Second, for individuals
considered part of Trump's electoral base – either past Trump voters or
Republicans – immigration is even more important to their vote choice.
Finally, cultural threat also drives how important immigration could potentially
be for voters in 2020.

Taking into consideration both the public salience of the issue and Trump's
focus on it, it is likely that voters will hold him accountable for his behavior in
this policy area. His base supporters will probably focus on whether he
delivered on campaign promises to build a border wall and restrict immigration,
while liberal or Democratic voters may be more focused on whether his
immigration policies have caused harm to specific racial and ethnic groups, as
well as whether they view his statements and behaviors on immigration to be
racist. To examine public perceptions of Trump's performance on immigration,
we asked respondents, "Do you approve or disapprove of the way President
Trump is handling the issue of immigration?" Answer choices included a range
from "Strongly Approve" to "Strongly Disapprove." Across the entire sample,

59 percent of respondents strongly disapproved of the president's handling of immigration, and another 13 percent somewhat disapproved.

These numbers are markedly different, however, when one focuses on partisan differences and past Trump voters. A total of 4 percent of Democrats expressed approval of Trump's job on immigration, with less than 1 percent indicating strong support. Among Republicans, on the other hand, 36 percent strongly approved of the president's job on immigration, and another 37 percent somewhat approved, totaling 73 percent approval. Past Trump voters were more fervent in their approval, with 40 percent expressing strong approval and another 38 percent indicating that they somewhat approved, for a total of 78 percent approval. Similarly, among those with high levels of cultural threat, 32 percent expressed strong support and another 36 percent somewhat approved of the president's performance on immigration. Support for Trump's behavior on immigration, then, is not uniformly high. Nearly 40 percent of Republicans, past Trump voters, and those with heightened levels of cultural threat only somewhat approved. This lower level of enthusiasm for Trump's record on immigration may be partially driven by Trump's inability to deliver on many of his campaign promises, as no major legislation has been enacted in this area.

Immigration will likely be a critical factor for how people choose to vote in 2020 and beyond, particularly among key elements of the Republican base, and it is important for political observers to consider how candidates frame their positions and appeals on the issue. Hence, we expect Trump, in order to provoke high turnout from the segments of the electorate who are nativist and racist, to ramp up his anti-immigrant rhetoric and actions as the election nears.

5.4 Conclusion

Immigration is notoriously said to be "the third rail of American politics" (Nicholas 2010). The metaphor is fitting, and not solely because it is a politically charged and potentially dangerous issue for many elected officials to touch. In addition to their economic and environmental consequences, US immigration laws are often literally a matter of life and death, primarily for thousands of Latino migrants. The findings presented in this Element capture how many of these dynamics are playing out in the time of Trump. The good news is that white people overwhelmingly oppose the president's most punitive immigration policies. They are on the side of migrant rights advocates when it comes to Trump's border fortification, child detention, and family separation practices. The bad news is that some segments of the public strongly support such policies, and their attitudes are significantly motivated not only by political party, but also by racial resentment and feelings of cultural and demographic threat. This leads us to the ugly news, which is that receiving factual information about the harmful effects of Trump's immigration enforcement policies does not seem to move opinions.

What are the implications of these results, and what do they reveal about us as a nation? The racial anxieties triggered by and reflected in a country's immigration laws convey a great deal about its moral compass and how it comprehends its demographic past, present, and desired future (Ngai 2004; Zolberg 2006; Johnson 2007). Regrettably, as Nevins (2010) explains, the perceived need for immigration enforcement measures in the United States has historically been informed by "notions of racial purity and fears" of "race suicide," among other factors (67). These dynamics are most tellingly on display in when and how nations justify their building of border bulwarks and filling of migrant detention facilities. That racism continues to play a role in shaping opinions about anti-immigrant walls and cages helps explicate why white demographic and cultural fragility are activated by Trump's nativist actions and are fundamental to his presidential agenda and reelection campaign.

A final important takeaway of this Element is that white people who acknowledge their racial privilege and believe immigrants are highly discriminated against, have the potential to join with migrant communities and serve as a counterweight to the nativists who compose the president's racist electoral base. The vast majority of progressive whites already oppose the immigration laws and practices discussed in this study. Whether their policy preferences will result in political action remains to be seen and – regardless of who wins the White House come November – will determine how history will judge this generation of white Americans.

References

Abrajano, M., & Hajnal, Z. L. (2015). *White Backlash: Immigration, Race, and American Politics*, Princeton: Princeton University Press.

Acevedo, N. (2019). Why are migrant children dying in U.S. custody? *NBCNews*, May 29, www.nbcnews.com/news/latino/why-are.

Ackerman, A., & Furman, R. (2013). The criminalization of immigration and the privatization of the immigration detention: Implications for justice. *Contemporary Justice Review*, 16(2),251–263.

Agamben, G. (1998). *Homo Sacer: Sovereign Power and Bare Life*, Stanford, CA: Stanford University Press.

Alba, R., & Nee, V. (2003). *Remaking the American Mainstream: Assimilation and Contemporary Immigrants*, Cambridge: Harvard University Press.

American Academy of Pediatrics. (2018). AAP Statement Opposing the Border Security and Immigration Reform Act. *American Academy of Pediatrics*, www .aap.org/en-us/about-the-aap/aap-pressroom/Pages/AAPStatementOpposingBor derSecurityandImmigrationReformAct.aspx.

American Immigration Council. (2016). Aggravated felonies: An overview, 16 December, www.americanimmigrationcouncil.org/research/aggravated-felonies-overview.

American Immigration Council. (n.d.) Challenging unconstitutional conditions in CBP detention facilities, www.americanimmigrationcouncil.org/litiga tion/challenging-unconstitutional-conditions-cbp-detention-facilities.

American National Election Studies, University of Michigan, and Stanford University. (2017). *ANES 2016 Time Series Study*. Ann Arbor, MI: Inter-university Consortium for Political and Social Research [distributor], 2017–09-19. https://doi.org/10.3886/ICPSR36824.v2.

American National Election Studies, University of Michigan, and Stanford University. (2018).*ANES 2018 Pilot Study*. Ann Arbor, MI: Inter-university Consortium for Political and Social Research [distributor], https://election studies.org/data-center/2018-pilot-study/.

Andersson, R. (2014). *Illegality, Inc.: Clandestine Migration and the Business of Bordering Europe*, Los Angeles: University of California Press.

Andreas P. (2000a). *Border Games: Policing the U.S.–Mexico Divide*, Ithaca: Cornell University Press.

Andreas, P. (2000b). Introduction: The Wall after the Wall. In P. Andreas & T. Snyder, eds., *The Wall around the West: State Borders and Immigration Controls in North American and Europe*, New York: Rowman & Littlefield.

Applied Research Center. (2011). Shattered families: The perilous intersection of immigration enforcement and the child welfare system, November, www.raceforward.org/research/reports/shattered-families.

Argueta, C. (2016). *Border Security: Immigration Enforcement Between Ports of Entry*, Congressional Research Service.

Associated Press. (2019). More than 5,400 children split at border, according to new count. *NBC News*, www.nbcnews.com/news/us-news/more-5–400-children-split-border-according-new-count-n1071791.

Berinsky, A. J. (2009). *In Time of War: Understanding American Public Opinion from World War II to Iraq*, Chicago: University of Chicago Press.

Bogado, A. Doctor giving migrant children psychotropic drugs lost certification years ago. *Reveal*, www.revealnews.org/blog/exclusive-shiloh-doctor-lost-board-certification-to-treat-children-years-ago/.

Boswell, C. (2009). *The Political Uses of Expert Knowledge: Immigration Policy and Social Research*, Cambridge: Cambridge University Press.

Bosworth, M., & Kaufman, E. (2011). Foreigners in a carceral age: Immigration and imprisonment in the United States. *Law & Policy Review*, 22(2),429–454.

Brader, T., Valentino, N. A., & Suhay, E. (2008) What triggers public opposition to immigration? Anxiety, group cues, and immigration threat. *American Journal of Political Science*, 52(4),959–978.

Branton, R. P., et al. (2007). Anglo voting on nativist ballot initiatives: The partisan impact of spatial proximity to the US-Mexico border. *Social Science Quarterly*, 88(3),882–897.

Brown, W. (2017). *Walled States, Waning Sovereignty*, New York: Zone.

Byman, D. (2019). Right-wingers are America's deadliest terrorists. *Slate*, https://slate.com/news-and-politics/2019/08/right-wing-terrorist-killings-government-focus-jihadis-islamic-radicalism.html.

Campbell, D., & Stanley, J. (1966) *Experimental and Quasi-Experimental Designs for Research*, Boston: Houghton Mifflin Company.

Calavita, K. (1996). The new politics of immigration: "Balanced-budget conservativism" and the Symbolism of Proposition 187. *Social Problems*, 43 (3),284–305.

Calder, B. J., Phillips, L. W., & Tybout, A. M. (1982). The concept of external validity. *Journal of Consumer Research*, 9(3),240–244.

Cantor, G. (2015). *Hieleras* (iceboxes) in the Rio Grande Valley sector. *American Immigration Council*, www.americanimmigrationcouncil.org/research/hieleras-iceboxes-rio-grande-valley-sector.

Carter, D. B., & Poast, P. (2017). Why do states build walls? Political economy, security, and border stability. *Journal of Conflict Resolution*, 61(2):239–270.

Carter, N. (2019). *American while Black: African Americans, Immigration, and the Limits of Citizenship*, New York: Oxford University Press.

Casellas, J. P., & Wallace, S. J. (2019). Sanctuary cities: Public attitudes towards enforcement collaboration. *Urban Affairs Review*, https://doi.org/10.1177% 2F1078087418776115,

CBS News. (2019). "I was separated from him. I was taken": A 7-year-old torn from her father at the U.S. border. *CBS News*, www.cbsnews.com/news/ faces-of-family-separation-cbsn-originals-documentary/.

Chacon, J. (2013). The security myth: Punishing immigrants in the name of national security. In J. Dowling & J. X. Inda, eds., *Governing Immigration through Crime: A Reader*, Stanford, CA: Stanford University Press.

Chacon, J. (2014). Immigration detention: No turning back? *South Atlantic Review*, 113(3),621–628.

Chapin, A. (2019). Four severely ill migrant toddlers hospitalized after lawyers visit border patrol facility. *Huffpost*, www.huffpost.com/entry/four-severely-ill-migrant-babies-hospitalized-after-lawyers-visited-border-patrol-facility _n_5d0d3bbce4b07ae90d9cfe4f.

Chavez, L. (2001). *Covering Immigration: Popular Images and the Politics of the Nation*, Los Angeles: University of California Press.

Chavez, L. (2008). *The Latino Threat: Constructing Immigrants, Citizens, and the Nation*, Stanford: Stanford University Press.

Chen, A., & Gill, J. (2015). Unaccompanied children and the U.S. immigration system: Challenges and reforms. *Journal of International Affairs*, 68 (2),115–133.

Chen, M. K., & Shapiro, J. M. (2007) Do harsher prison conditions reduce recidivism? A discontinuity-based approach. *American Law and Economics Review*, 9(1):1–29.

Chiacu, D., & Lynch, S.N. (2018). Trump says illegal immigrants should be deported with "No judges or court cases." *Reuters*, www.reuters.com/article/ us-usa.

Chishti, M., & Hipsman, F. (2015). The child and family migration surge of summer 2014: A short-lived crisis with lasting impacts. *Journal of International Affairs*, 68(2),95–114.

Chotiner, I. (2019). How the stress of separation and detention changes the lives of children. *New Yorker*, www.newyorker.com/news/q-and-a/how-the-stress-of-separation-and-detention-changes-the-lives-of-children.

Cillizza, C. (2018). Donald Trump just said something truly terrifying. *CNN*, 25 July 2018, www.cnn.com/2018/07/25/politics/donald-trump-vfw-unreality/index.html.

Citrin, J., & Sides, J. (2008). Immigration and the imagined community in Europe and the United States. *Political Studies*, 56(1),33–56.

Citrin, J., et al. (1997). Public opinion toward immigration reform: The role of economic motivations. *The Journal of Politics*, 59(3),858–881.

Clark, A. B. (2017). Juvenile solitary confinement as a form of child abuse. *The Journal of the American Academy of Psychiatry and the Law*, 45 (3),350–357.

Cochrane, E. (2019). The House and Senate have separate plans for border aid. Here's what's different. *The New York Times*, www.nytimes.com/2019/06/24/us/politics/house-senate.

Cohn, J. (2007). The environmental impacts of a border fence. *BioScience*, 57 (1), 96.

Coleman, M. (2012). The 'local' migration state: The site-specific devolution of immigration enforcement in the U.S. south. *Law & Policy*, 34 (2),159–190.

Coleman, M. & Kocher, A. (2011). Detention, deportation, devolution and immigrant incapacitation in the US, post 9/11, *The Geographical Journal*, 177(3),228–237.

Collingwood, L., Morin, J., & El-Khatib, S. O. (2018). Expanding carceral markets: Detention facilities, ICE contracts, and the financial interests of punitive immigration policy, *Race and Social Problems*, DOI:10.1007/s1255201892415.

Conlon, D., & N. Hiemstra. (2014). Examining the everyday micro-economies of migrant detention in the United States, *Geographic Helvetica*, 69, 335–344.

Cornelisse, G. (2010). Immigration detention and the territoriality of universal rights. In N. De Genova & N. Peutz, eds., *The Deportation Regime: Sovereignty, Space, and the Freedom of Movement*, Durham: Duke University Press.

Cornelius, W. A. (2005). Controlling "unwanted" immigration: Lessons from the United States, 1993–2004. *Journal of Ethnic and Migration Studies*, 31 (4),775–794.

Cortina, J. (2019). From a distance: Geographic proximity, partisanship, and public attitudes toward the U.S.–Mexico border wall. *Political Research Quarterly*, DOI:10.1177/1065912919854135.

Coutin, S. B. (2010). Confined within: National territories as zones of confinement, *Political Geography*, 29, 200–2008.

Cox, A., & Goodman, R. (2018). Detention of migrant families as "deterrence": Ethical flaws and empirical doubts. https://perma.cc/Q5S6-WELR.

da Silva, C. (2019). Trump has built nearly 100 miles of border wall by end of 2019, with 350 miles to go in 2020. *Newsweek*, www.newsweek.com/donald-trump-border-wall-u-s-mexico-2020-goal-1479821.

da Silva, C. (2020). ICE accused of using coronavirus crisis to launch "Family Separation 2.0." *Newsweek*, www.newsweek.com/ice-accused-using-coronavirus-crisis-launch-family-separation-2–0-1505156.

Davila-Ruhaak, S., Schwinn, S., & Chan, J. (2014). Concerning the United States mistreatment of immigrant detainees in violation of the convention against torture and other cruel, inhuman or degrading treatment of punishment. Joint Submission to the U.N. Committee Against Torture, John Marshall Law School.

Davis, J. H., & Shears, M. D. (2019). *Border Wars*, New York: Simon and Schuster.

De Genova, N. (2007). The production of culprits: From deportability to detainability in the aftermath of "homeland security." *Citizenship Studies*, 11(5),421–448.

De Genova, N. (2017). The economy of detainability: Theorizing migrant detention. In M. Flynn & M. Flynn, eds., *Challenging Immigrant Detention: Academics, Activists, and Policy-makers*, Northampton, MA: Edward Elgar Publishing.

De Leon, J. (2015). *The Land of Open Graves: Living and Dying on the Migrant Trail*, Los Angeles: University of California Press.

DEA. (2018). *2018 National Drug Threat Assessment*, U.S. Department of Justice Drug Enforcement Administration.

Dear, M. (2013). *Why Walls Won't Work*, New York: Oxford University Press.

Delli Carpini, M., & Keeter, S. (1996). *What Americans Know about Politics and Why it Matters*. New Haven: Yale University Press.

Department of Justice. (2020). The Department of Justice creates section dedicated to denaturalization of cases. *Department of Justice Office of Public Affairs*, 26 February, www.justice.gov/opa/pr/department-justice-creates-section-dedicated-denaturalization-cases.

Dickerson, C. (2019). "There is a stench": Soiled clothes and no baths for migrant children at a Texas center. *New York Times*, www.nytimes.com /2019/06/21/us/migrant-children-border-soap.html.

Dickerson, C. (2019). The youngest child separated from his family at the border was 4 months old. *New York Times*, www.nytimes.com/2019/06/16/ us/baby-constantine-romania-migrants.html.

Dickerson, C. (2019). No more hieleras: Doe v. Kelly's fight for constitutional rights at the border. *The New York Times*, www.nytimes.com/2019/06/21/us/ migrant-children.

Dimcock, M. (2019). An update on our research into trusts, facts, and democracy. Pew Research Center, www.pewresearch.org/2019/06/05/an-update.

Doe v. Johnson. United States District Court, (2015).

Doe v. Kelly. Uniter States Court of Appeals for the Ninth Circuit, (2017).

Doe v. Nielsen. United States District Court, (2019).

Doe vs. Wolf. United States District Court, (2015).

Domonoske, C., & Gonzalez, R. (2018). What we know: Family separation and "zero tolerance" at the border. *NPR,* www.npr.org/2018/06/19/621065383/ what-we-know-family-separation-and-zero-tolerance-at-the-border.

Doty, R. L., & Wheatley, E. S. (2013). Private detention and the immigration industrial complex. *International Political Sociology,* 7, 426–443.

Dow, M. (2005). *American Gulag: Inside U.S. Immigration Prisons,* Los Angeles: University of California Press.

Druckman, J. N., et al. (2011). *Cambridge Handbook of Experimental Political Science,* New York: Cambridge University Press.

Dunaway, J., Branton, R. P., & Abrajano, M. (2010). Agenda setting, public opinion, and the issue of immigration reform. *Social Science Quarterly,* 91(2),359–378.

Dunn, T. (1996). *The Militarization of the U.S.–Mexico Border, 1978–1992,* Austin: University of Texas Press.

Echavarri, F. (2019). Border patrol's toxic culture goes way beyond Facebook groups: It's actually for sale on a t-shirt. *Mother Jones,* www.motherjones.com /politics/2019/07/border-patrol-racist-texts-bowen-t-shirt/.

Economist/YouGov. (2018). Economist/YouGov poll, 3–5 June, https:// d25d2506sfb94s.cloudfront.net/cumulus_uploads/document/dtt00zl5up/ econTabReport.pdf.

Enchautegui, M., & Menjivar, C. (2015). Paradoxes of family immigration policy: Separation, reorganization, and reunification of families under current immigration laws. *Law & Policy,* 37(1–2), 32–60.

Eriksson, L., & Taylor, M. (2008). The environmental impacts of the border wall between Texas and Mexico. University of Texas School of Law Working Group on Human Rights and the Border Wall Report to the Organization of American States.

Escobar, M. (2016). *Captivity beyond Prisons: Criminalization Experiences of Latina (Im)Migrants,* Austin: University of Texas Press.

Espenshade, T. J., Baraka, J. L., & Huber, G. A. (1997) Implications of the 1996 Welfare and Immigration Reform Acts for US immigration. *Population and Development Review,* 23(4),769–801.

Felbab-Brown, V. (2017). The Wall: The real costs of a barrier between the United States and Mexico. *Brookings,* www.brookings.edu/essay/the-wall-the-real-costs-of-a-barrier-between-the-united-states-and-mexico/.

Fernandes, D. (2007). *Targeted: Homeland Security and the Business of Immigration,* New York: Seven Stories Press.

Fernandez, M. (2019). Lawyer draws outrage for defending lack of tooth-brushes in border detention. *The New York Times*, www.nytimes.com/2019/06/25/us/sarah-fabian.

Filipovic, J. (2019). Adoption of separated migrant kids shows "pro-life" groups' disrespect for maternity. *Guardian*, www.theguardian.com/commentisfree/2019/oct/30/adoption-separated-migrant-children-pro-lifers-deep-disrespect-for-maternity.

Fix, M., & Zimmerman, W. (1997). Welfare reform: A new immigrant policy for the United States. http://webarchive.urban.org/publications/407532.html

Flagg, A. (2019). Is there a connection between undocumented immigrants and crime? *The New York Times*, www.nytimes.com/2019/05/13/upshot/illegal-immigration.

Flores v. Reno. 507 U.S. 292, (1993).

Flynn, D. J., Nyhan, B., & Reifler, J. (2017). The nature and origins of misperceptions: understanding false and unsupported beliefs about politics. *Political Psychology*, 38(1),127–150.

Flynn, M. (2017). Capitalism and immigration control: What political economy reveals about the global spread of detention. In M. Flynn & M. Flynn, eds., *Challenging Immigrant Detention: Academics, Activists, and Policy-makers*, Northampton, MA: Edward Elgar Publishing.

Flynn, M., & Flynn, M. (2017). Critiquing zones of exception: Actor-orientated approaches explaining the rise of immigration detention. In D. Brotherton & P. Kretsedemas, eds., *Immigration Policy in the Age of Punishment: Detention, Deportation, and Border Control*, New York: Columbia University Press.

Fraga, L. R., et al. (2011) *Latinos in the New Millennium: An Almanac of Opinion, Behavior, and Policy Preferences*, New York: Cambridge University Press.

Frazee, G., & Barajas, J. (2019). Trump says walls work. It's much more complicated. *PBS Newshour*, www.pbs.org/newshour/nation/trump-says.

Freking, K., & Spagat, E. (2019). Trump calls the new border wall a "world-class security system." *Time Magazine*, https://time.com/5680944/trump-border.

Funk, C., Heffron, M., Kennedy, B., & Johnson, C. (2019). Trust and Mistrust in Americans' Views of Scientific Experts. Pew Research Center, https://www.pewresearch.org/science/2019/08/02/trust-and-mistrust-in-americans-views-of-scientific-experts/

Gadarian, S. K., & Albertson, B. (2014). Anxiety, immigration, and the search for information. *Political Psychology*, 35(2),133–164.

GAO. (2006). Border-crossing deaths have doubled since 1995; Border Patrol's efforts to prevent deaths have not been fully evaluated. United States Government Accountability Office.

Garcia Hernandez, C.C. (2014). Immigration Detention as Punishment. *UCLA Law Review*, 61 (5), 1346–1415.

Garcia Hernandez, C. C. (2019). *Migrating to Prison: America's Obsession with Locking Up Immigrants*, New York: The New Press.

Garret, T. (2009). The border fence, immigration policy, and the Obama administration: A cautionary note. *Administrative Theory & Praxis*, 32(1),129–133.

Gerstein J., & Hesson, T. (2018). Federal judge orders Trump administration to reunite migrant families. *Politico*, www.politico.com/story/2018/06/26/judge-orders-trump-reunite-migrant-families-678809.

Gilens, M. (1999) *Why Americans Hate Welfare*, Chicago: University of Chicago Press.

Gilens, M. (2001). Political ignorance and collective policy preferences. *American Political Science Review*, 95(2),379–396.

Gilman, D. (2011). Seeking breaches in the wall: An international human rights law challenge to the Texas–Mexico border wall, *Texas International Law Journal*, 46, 257–293.

Golash-Boza, T. (2009). The immigration industrial complex: Why we enforce immigration policies destined to fail, *Sociological Compass*, 3)2), 295–309.

Golash-Boza, T. (2015). *Deported: Immigrant Policing, Disposable Labor and Global Capitalism*, New York: New York University Press.

Gonzales, R. (2019). Sexual assault of detained migrant children reported in the thousands since 2015. *NPR*, www.npr.org/2019/02/26/698397631/sexual-assault-of-detained-migrant-children-reported-in-the-thousands-since-2015.

Gonzales, R. (2019). ACLU: Administration is still separating migrant families despite court order to stop. *NPR*, www.npr.org/2019/07/30/746746147/aclu-administration-is-still-separating-migrant-families-despite-court-order-to-/.

Golunov, S. (2014). Border fences in the globalizing world: Beyond traditional geopolitics and post-positivist approaches. In E. Vallet, ed., *Borders, Fences and Walls*, New York: Routledge.

Graham, D. A., et al. (2019) An oral history of Trump's bigotry. *The Atlantic*, www.theatlantic.com/magazine/archive/2019/06/trump-racism.

Grandin, G. (2019). *How the U.S. weaponized the border wall. The Intercept*, https://theintercept.com/2019/02/10/us-mexico-border-fence-history/.

Gravelle, T. (2016) Party identification, contact, contexts, and public attitudes toward illegal immigration. *Public Opinion Quarterly*, 80(1),1–25.

Gravelle, T. (2018). Politics, time, space, and attitudes toward US–Mexico border security. *Political Geography*, 65(July), 107–116.

Guenther, L. (2013). *Solitary Confinement: Social Death and Its Afterlives*, Minneapolis: University of Minnesota Press.

Haddal, C., Kim, Y., & Garcia, M. J. (2009). Border security: Barriers along the U.S. international border. Congressional Research Service.

Hainmueller, J., & Hiscox, M. J. (2007). Educated preferences: Explaining attitudes toward immigration in Europe. *International Organization*, 61(2),399–442.

Hainmueller, J., & Hiscox, M. J. (2010). Attitudes toward highly skilled and low-skilled immigration: Evidence from a survey experiment. *American Political Science Review*, 104(1),61–84.

Hainmueller, J., & Hopkins, D. J. (2014). Public attitudes toward immigration. *Annual Review of Political Science*, 17, 225–249.

Hajnal, Z., & Rivera, M. U. (2014) Immigration, Latinos, and white partisan politics: The new Democratic defection. *American Journal of Political Science*, 58(4),773–789.

Hanson, G., Scheve K., & Slaughter, M. (2009). Individual Preferences over High-Skilled Immigration in the United States. In J. Bhagwati & G. Hanson, eds., *Skilled Immigration Today: Problems, Prospects, and Policies*, New York: Oxford University Press.

Harvey, D. (2007). *A Brief History of Neoliberalism*, New York: Oxford University Press.

Hasan, M. (2019). After El Paso, we can no longer ignore Trump's Role in inspiring mass shootings. *The Intercept*, https://theintercept.com/2019/08/04/el-paso-dayton-mass-shootings-donald-trump/.

Hassner, R., & Wittenberg, J. (2015). Barriers to entry: Who builds fortified boundaries and why?. *International Security*, 40(1),157–190.

Hayden, M. E. (2019). Stephen Miller's affinity for white nationalism revealed in leaked emails. *Hatewatch*, www.splcenter.org/hatewatch/2019/11/12/stephen-millers-affinity-white-nationalism-revealed-leaked-emails.

Haynes, C., Merolla, J., & Ramakrishnan, S. K. (2016). *Framing Immigrants: News Coverage, Public Opinion, and Policy*, New York: Russell Sage Foundation.

Hernandez, D. (2019). Carceral shadows: Entangled Lineages and Technologies of Migrant Detention. In R. Chase, ed., *Caging Borders and Carceral States: Incarcerations, Immigration Detentions, and Resistance*, Chapel Hill: University of North Carolina Press.

Herweck, S., & Nicol, S. (2018). Death, damage, and failure: Past, present, and future impacts of walls on the U.S.–Mexico border. ACLU Border Rights Center.

Hesson, T., & Rosenberg, M. (2020). U.S. deports 400 migrant children under new coronavirus rules. *Reuters*, www.reuters.com/article/us-health-coronavirus-usa-deportations-idUSKBN21P354?fbclid=IwAR1EF-OAPOHU1fWSVm02B-0iVI8dqUaU9hT5XVrtiQeJ8TNJXUd2-prgOmE.

Heyman, J. M. (2008) Constructing a virtual wall: Race and citizenship in US–Mexico border policing. *Journal of the Southwest*, 50(3),305–333.

Hiemstra, N. (2014). Performing homeland security within the US immigration detention system. *Environment and Planning D: Society and Space*, 32, 571–588.

Hiemstra, N. (2019). *Detain and Deport: The Chaotic U.S. Immigration Enforcement Regime*, Athens: University of Georgia Press.

Hing, B. O. (2019). *American Presidents, Deportations, and Human Rights Violations: From Carter to Trump*, New York: Cambridge University Press.

Hirschfeld Davis, J., & Shear, M. D. (2019). *Border Wars: Inside Trump's Assault on Immigration*, New York: Simon & Schuster.

Hiskey, C., Malone, M., & Orces, D. (2018). Leaving the devil you know: Crime victimization, U.S. deterrence policy, and the emigration decisions in Central America. *Latin American Research Review*, 53, 429–47.

Hochschild, A. R. (2018). *Strangers in Their Own Land*, New York: The New Press.

Holpuch, A. (2019). Thousands more migrant children separated under Trump than previously known. *Guardian*, www.theguardian.com/us-news/2019/jan/17/trump-family-separations-report-latest-news-zero-tolerance-policy-immigrant-children.

Hooghe, M., & Dassonneville, R. (2018). Explaining the Trump vote: The effect of racist resentment and anti-immigrant sentiments. *PS*, 51(3),528–534.

Hopkins, D. J. (2010) Politicized places: Explaining where and when immigrants provoke local opposition. *American Political Science Review*, 104 (1),40–60.

Hopkins, D. J., Sides, J., & Citrin, J. (2019) The muted consequences of correct information about immigration. *Journal of Politics*, 81(1),315–320.

Human Rights First. (2018). The Flores settlement and family incarceration: A brief history and next steps. 30 October. www.humanrightsfirst.org/resource/flores-settlement-and-family-incarceration-brief-history-and-next-steps.

Inda, J. X. (2013). Subject to deportation: IRCA, 'criminal aliens,' and the policing of immigration. *Migration Studies*, 1(3),292–310.

Ipsos. (2018). Americans' views on immigration policy. 15 June, www.ipsos.com/en-us/news-polls/americans-views-on-immigration-policy.

International Organization for Migration. (2020). Total of deaths recorded in U.S.–Mexico border in 2020. *Missing Migrant Project*. Accessed March 10, https://missingmigrants.iom.int/region/americas?region=1422.

Jacobson, G. (2017). The triumph of polarized partisanship in 2016: Donald Trump's improbable victory. *Political Science Quarterly*, 132(1), DOI:10.1002/polq.12572.

Jacobson, M. F. (1998). *Whiteness of a Different Color: European Immigrants and the Alchemy of Race*, Cambridge, MA: Harvard University Press.

Jardina, A. (2019). *White Identity Politics*, New York: Cambridge University Press.

Jerit, J., & Zhao, Y. (2020). Political misinformation. *Annual Review of Political Science*, 23, 77–94.

Johnson, K. R. (2004). *The "Huddled Masses" Myth: Immigration and Civil Rights*, Philadelphia: Temple University Press.

Johnson, K. R. (2007). *Opening the Floodgates: Why America Needs to Rethink Its Borders and Immigration Laws*, New York: New York University Press.

Jones-Correa, M., & de Graauw, E. (2013). The illegality trap: The politics of immigration & the lens of Illegality. *Daedalus*, 142(3),185–198.

Jones, R. (2012). *Border Walls: Security and the War on Terror in the United States, India, and Israel*, New York: Zed Books.

Jones, R. (2017). *Violent Borders: Refugees and the Right to Move*, New York: Verso Press.

Jones, R., & Johnson, C. (2016). Border militarisation and the re-articulation of sovereignty. *Transactions of the Institute of British Geographers*, 41(2),187–200.

Joyce, K. (2018). The threat of international adoption for migrant children separated from their families. *The Intercept*, theintercept.com/2018/07/01/separated-children-adoption-immigration/.

Juarez, M., Gomez-Aguinaga, B., & Betteez S. (2018). Twenty years after IRCA: The rise of immigrant detention and its effects on Latinx communities across the nation. *Journal on Migration and Human Security*, 6(1),74–96.

Junn, J. (2017). The Trump majority: White womanhood and the making of female voters in the US. *Politics, Groups, and Identities*, 5(2),343–352.

Kahn, R. (1996). *Other People's Blood: U.S. Immigration Prisons in the Reagan Decade*, Boulder: Westview Press.

Kandel, W. (2017). *Unaccompanied Alien Children: An Overview*, Congressional Research Service.

Kanno-Youngs, Z. (2019). Poor conditions persist for migrant children detained at the border, Democrats say. *The New York Times*, www.nytimes.com/2019/08/29/us/politics/homeland-security.

Kanstroom, D. (2007). *Deportation Nation: Outsiders in American History*, Cambridge: Harvard University Press.

Katz, J. (2019). Op-ed: Call immigrant detention centers what they really are: Concentration camps. *Los Angeles Times*, www.latimes.com/opinion/op-ed/la. June 9.

Katz, L., Levitt, S. D., & Shustorovich, E. (2003). Prison conditions, capital punishment, and deterrence. *American Law and Economics Review*, 5(2),318–343.

Kendi, I. X. (2019). The day *shithole* entered the presidential lexicon. *Atlantic*, www.theatlantic.com/politics/archive/2019/01/shithole-countries /580054/.

Kilani, H. (2019). The walls fall: Prototypes for Trump's southern border barrier come down. *Guardian*, www.theguardian.com/us-news/2019/feb/28/trump-border-wall-mexico-prototypes-demolition.

Kinder, D. R., & Kam, C. D. (2010) *Us against them: Ethnocentric Foundations of American Opinion*, Chicago: University of Chicago Press.

Kinder, D. R., & Sanders, L. M. (1996). *Divided by Color*, Chicago: University of Chicago Press.

King, D. S., & Smith, R. M. (2005). Racial orders in American political development. *American Political Science Review*, 99(1),75–92.

Kirby, J. (2018). President Trump wants fewer immigrants from 'shithole countries' and more from places like Norway. *Vox*, www.vox.com/platform/amp/ 2018/1/11/16880750/trump-immigrants-shithole-countries-norway.

Koerner, C. (2019). Kids describe in their own words the dire conditions inside a border detention center. *BuzzFeed News*, 27 July, www.buzzfeednews.com/ article/claudiakoerner/children-border-detention-conditions-immigrants-hungry.

Korte G., & Gomez, A. (2018). Trump ramps up rhetoric on undocumented immigrants: "These aren't people. These are animals." *USA Today*, https://eu .usatoday.com/story/news/politics/2018/05/16/trump-immigrants-animals-mexico-democrats-sanctuary-cities/617252002/.

Krysan, M. (2000) Prejudice, politics, and public opinion: Understanding the sources of racial policy attitudes. *Annual review of sociology*, 26 (1),135–168.

Kuklinski, J. H., et al. (1997) Racial prejudice and attitudes toward affirmative action. *American Journal of Political Science*, 41(2),402–419.

Kuklinski, J. H., et al. (2000). Misinformation and the currency of democratic citizenship. *Journal of Politics*, 62(3),790–816.

Kumar, A. (2020) After delays, Trump on track to build more than 450 miles of border wall. *Politico*, February 14, www.politico.com/news/2020/02/14/ trump-450.

Layman, G. C., Carsey, T. M., & Horowitz, J. M. (2006). Party polarization in American politics: Characteristics, causes, and consequences. *Annual Review of Political Science*, 9, 83–110.

Lazer, D. M. J., et al. (2018) The science of fake news. *Science*, 359 (638),1094–1096.

Lee, E. (2019). *America for Americans: A History of Xenophobia in the United States*, New York: Basic Books.

Lee, J. (2016). Lonely too long: Redefining and reforming juvenile solitary confinement. *Fordham Law Review*, 85(2),845–876.

Lee, M. Y. H. (2015) Donald Trump's false comments connecting Mexican immigrants and crime. *Washington Post*. July 8. www.washingtonpost.com /news/fact-checker/wp/2015/07/08/donald-trumps-false-comments-connecting-mexican-immigrants-and-crime/.

Lee, S. (2019). Family separation as slow death, *Columbia Law Review*, 119 (8),2320–2384.

Leiken, R., & Brooke, S. (2006). The quantitative analysis of terrorism and immigration: An initial exploration. *Terrorism and Political Violence*, 18 (4),503–521.

Leonhardt, D., et al. (2018). Donald Trump's racism: The definitive list, updated. *The New York Times*, www.nytimes.com/interactive/2018/01/15/ opinion/leonhardt-trump-racist.html.

Levine, M., & Arkin, J. (2019) Republicans support Trump's wall even after he grabs military funds from their states. *Politico*, September 11, www .politico.com/story/2019/09/11/republicans-border.

Light, M. T., & Miller, T. (2018). Does undocumented immigration increase violent crime? *Criminology*, 56(2),370–401.

Lind, D., & Scott, D. (2018). Flores agreement: Trump's executive order to end family separation might run afoul of a 1997 court ruling. *Vox*, www.vox.com /2018/6/20/17484546/executive-order.

Linton, J. M., Griffin, M., & Shapiro, A. J. (2017). Detention of immigrant children. *Pediatrics*, 139, e20170483.

Liptak, K. (2019). Trump warns of "crisis of the heart" in immigration address. *CNN*, www.cnn.com/2019/01/08/politics/donald-trump.

Long, C. (2019). Written testimony submitted to the U.S. House Committee on Oversight and Reform Subcommittee on Civil Rights and Civil Liberties for hearing on: "Kids in Cages: Inhumane Treatment at the Border." Human Rights Watch.

Long, C., & Mukherjee, E. (2019). The whole child separation travesty is pointless. *CNN*, www.cnn.com/2019/08/07/opinions/the-child.

Longo, M. (2018). *The Politics of Borders: Sovereignty Security, and the Citizen after 9/11*, Cambridge: Cambridge University press.

Lopez, G. (2019). Donald Trump's long history of racism, from the 1970s to 2019. *Vox*, www.vox.com/2016/7/25/12270880/donald-trump.

Lopez Bunyasi, T. (2015). Color-cognizance and color-blindness in White America: Perceptions of whiteness and their potential to predict racial policy attitudes at the dawn of the twenty-first century. *Sociology of Race and Ethnicity*, 1(2),209–224.

Lovato, R. (2019). Julián Castro and the Democrats' catastrophic accent (and immigration) problem. *Latino Rebels*, www.latinorebels.com/2019/01/14/castroproblems/.

Loyd, J., & Mountz, A. (2018). *Boats, Borders, and Bases: Race, the Cold War, and the Rise of Migration Detention in the United States*, Oakland: University of California Press.

Loyd, J., Mitchelson, M., & Burridge, A., eds. (2012). *Beyond Walls and Cages: Prisons, Borders, and Global Crisis*, Athens: University of Georgia Press.

Luibheid, E. (2002). *Entry Denied: Controlling Sexuality at the Border*, Minneapolis: University of Minnesota Press.

Lytle Hernandez, K. (2010). *Migra! A history of the U.S. Border Patrol*, Los Angeles: University of California Press.

Macias-Rojas, P. (2016). *From Deportation to Prison: The Politics of Immigration Enforcement in Post-Civil Rights America*, New York: New York University Press.

MacLean, S.A. l. (2019). Mental health of children held at a United States immigration detention center. *Social Science & Medicine*, 230(2),303–308.

Mainwaring, C. & Silverman, S. (2017). Detention-as-spectacle. *International Political Sociology*, 11, 21–38.

Malhotra, N., Margalit, Y. & Mo, C. H. (2013). Economic explanations for opposition to immigration: Distinguishing between prevalence and conditional Impact. *American Journal of Political Science*, 57(2),391–410.

Marquez-Avila, M. (2019). No more *hieleras*: Doe v. Kelly's fight for constitutional rights at the border. *UCLA L. Rev.*, 66, 818.

Martin, D. D. (2020). Trump has built just 1 mile of new border wall since taking office. *American Independent*, https://americanindependent.com/donald-trump-border-wall-1-mile-mexico-immigration-customs-and-border-protection-cbp/.

Martin J. (2020). 60 percent of ICE detainees tested have corona virus. *Newsweek*, www.newsweek.com/60-percent-ice-detainees-tested-have-coronavirus-1500817.

Martin, L. (2012a). "Catch and remove": Detention, deterrence, and discipline in US noncitizen family detention practice. *Geopolitics*, 17, 312–334.

Martin, L. (2012b). Governing through the family: Struggles over US noncitizen family detention policy. *Environment and Planning A*, 44, 886–888.

Martin, L. (2017a). Discretion, contracting, and commodification: Privatisation of US immigration detention as a technology of government. In D. Conlon & N. Hiemstra eds., *Intimate Economies of Immigration Detention: Critical Perspectives*, London: Routledge.

Martin, L. (2017b). Family detention, law, and geopolitics in US immigration enforcement policy. In C. Harker, K. Horschelmann, & T. Skelton, eds., *Geographies of Children and Young People: Conflict, Violence and Peace*, Vol. 11. Singapore: Springer.

Masuoka, N., & Junn, J. (2013). *The Politics of Belonging: Race, Public Opinion, and Immigration*, Chicago: University of Chicago Press.

Matthews, D. (2018) Polls: Trump's family separation policy is very unpopular – except among Republicans. *Vox*, www.vox.com/policy-and-politics /2018/6/18/17475740/family-separation-poll-polling-border-trump-children -immigrant-families-parents.

McDermott, R. (2011). Internal and external validity. In Jamie Druckman et al., eds., *Cambridge Handbook of Experimental Political Science*, New York: Oxford University Press. 27–40.

Menjivar, C., & Kanstroom, D. (2013). *Constructing Immigrant 'Illegality': Critiques, Experiences, and Responses*, New York: Cambridge University Press.

Mitchell, A., et al. (2019). Many Americans say made-up news is a critical problem that needs to be fixed. Pew Research Center, June, 5.

Mark, M. (2018). Trump just referred to one of his infamous campaign comments: Calling Mexicans "Rapists." *Business Insider*, www .businessinsider.com/trump-mexicans-rapists-remark-reference-2018-4.

Miroff, N. (2019). Smugglers are sawing through new sections of Trump's border wall. *Washington Post*, www.washingtonpost.com/national/smug glers-are-sawing-through-new-sections-of-trumps-border-wall/2019/11/01/ 25bf8ce0-fa72-11e9-ac8c-8eced29ca6ef_story.html?arc404=true.

Molina, N. (2014). *How Race Is Made in America: Immigration, Citizenship, and the Historical Power of Racial Scripts*, Los Angeles: University of California Press.

Montoya-Galvez, C. (2020). Chicago coronavirus outbreak infects dozens of migrant children in U.S. custody. *CBS News*, www.cbsnews.com/news/chi cago-coronavirus-outbreak-infects-dozens-of-migrant-children-in-us custody/? fbclid=IwAR1Gi45kyHcCkSQIK7ywE_Fai1KNLEoAcxtdZjoUvfZUMbL37- k2YAViO-jA.

Moreno, C. (2016). Nine outrageous things Donald Trump has said about Latinos. *Huffington Post*, www.huffpost.com/entry/9-outrageous-things- donald-trump-has-said-about-latinos_n_55e483a1e4b0c818f618904b.

Moreno, E. (2020). More than three dozen migrant children in Chicago shelters infected with coronavirus. *The Hill*, https://thehill.com/homenews/news/ 492718-more-than-three-dozen-migrant-children-in-chicago-shelters-infected -with.

Montini, E. J. (2019). Feds don't know locations of "thousands" more migrant kids, separated from families. *USA Today*, www.usatoday.com/story/opinion/2019/02/09/separation-immigrant-families-trump-thousands-column/2805714002/.

Nakamura, D. (2016). Flow of Central Americans to U.S. surging, expected to exceed 2014 numbers. *Washington Post*, www.washingtonpost.com/politics/flow-of-central-americans-to-us-surging-expected-to-exceed-2014-numbers/2016/09/22/ee127578-80da-11e6-8327-f141a7beb626_story.html.

Neeley, S. (2008). Immigration detention: The inaction of the Bureau of Immigration and Customs Enforcement. *Admin. L. Rev.*, 60, 729.

Nevins, J. (2010). *Operation Gatekeeper and Beyond: The War on "Illegals" and the Remaking of the U.S.–Mexico Boundary*, New York: Routledge.

Newman, B. J. (2013). Acculturating contexts and Anglo opposition to immigration in the United States. *American Journal of Political Science*, 57 (2),374–390.

Newman, D. (2006). The lines that continue to separate us: borders in our 'borderless' word. *Progress in Human Geography*, 30(2),143–161.

Newman, D., & Paasi, A. (1998). Fences and neighbours in the postmodern world: boundary narratives in political geography. *Progress in Human Geography*, 22(2),186–207.

Newman, L. K., & Steel, Z. (2008). The child asylum seeker: Psychological and developmental impact of immigration detention. *Child and Adolescent Psychiatric Clinics of North America*, 17(3),665–683.

Nicholas, P. (2010). Democrats point the finger at obama's chief of staff for immigration reform's poor progress. *Los Angeles Times*, www.latimes.com/archives/la-xpm-2010-may-21-la-na-immigration-20100521-story.html.

Nowrasteh, A. (2019). The cost of the border wall keeps climbing and it's becoming less of a wall. *Cato Institute*, www.cato.org/blog/cost-border-wall-keeps-climbing-its-becoming-less-wall.

Ngai, M. (2004). *Impossible Subjects: Illegal Aliens and the Making of Modern America*, Princeton: Princeton University Press.

Nguyen, T. (2018). The far-right rejoices as Trump says immigrants are destroying European "culture.: *Vanity Fair*, www.vanityfair.com/news/2018/07/donald-trump-culture-wars-britain.

Nieto-Gomez R. (2014). Walls, sensors and drones: Technology and surveillance on the US–Mexico Border. In E. Vallet, ed., *Borders, Fences and Walls*, New York: Routledge.

Noel, H. (2014). *Political Ideologies and Political Parties in America*, New York: Cambridge University Press.

Norman, J. (2019). Solid majority still opposes new construction on border wall. *Gallup*, https://news.gallup.com/poll/246455/solid-majority-opposes-new-construction-border-wall.aspx.

Norwaseth, A., & Orr, R. (2018). Immigration and the welfare state: Immigrant and native use rates and benefit levels for means-tested welfare and entitlement programs. *Cato Institute*, www.cato.org/publications/immigration-research.

Nowrasteh, A. (2019). Illegal immigrants and crime: Assessing the evidence. *Cato Institute*, www.cato.org/blog/illegal-immigrants-crime-assessing-evidence.

NPR. (2019). "Torture facilities": Eyewitnesses describe poor conditions at Texas detention centers for migrant children. *On Point*, NPR, June 25, www.wbur.org/onpoint/2019/06/25/texas-border-control-facilities-migrant-children.

Lind, D. (2019). The horrifying conditions facing kids in border detention, explained. *Vox*, www.vox.com/policy-and-politics/2019/6/25/18715725/children-border-detention-kids-cages-immigration.

Nyhan, B. (2010). Why the "death panel" myth wouldn't die: Misinformation in the health care reform debate. *The Forum*, 8(1).

Nyhan, B., & Reifler, J. (2010). When corrections fail: The persistence of political misperceptions. *Political Behavior*, 32(2),303–330.

Nyhan, B., & Reifler, J. (2015). Does correcting myths about the flu vaccine work? An experimental evaluation of the effects of corrective information. *Vaccine*, 33(3),459–464.

Nyhan, B., Reifler, J., & Ubel, P. A. (2013). The hazards of correcting myths about health care reform. *Medical care*, 51(2),127–132.

O'Dell, R. González, D., & Castellano, J. (2017). "Mass disaster" grows at the U.S.–Mexico border, but Washington doesn't seem to care. *AZCentral*, www.azcentral.com/story/news/politics/border-issues/2017/12/14/investigation-border-patrol-undercounts-deaths-border-crossing-migrants/933689001/.

O'Neil, E. (2018). Immigration issues: Public opinion on family separation, DACA, and a border wall. *AEI Blog*, www.aei.org/politics-and.

O'Toole, M., & Carcamo, C. (2020). Citing coronavirus, Trump officials refuse to release migrant kids to sponsors – and deport them instead. *Los Angeles Times*, www.latimes.com/politics/story/2020–05-12/trump-officials-coronavirus-refuse-releasing-migrant-kids.

Ohmae, K. (1999). *The Borderless World: Power and Strategy in the Interlinked Economy*, New York: HarperCollins.

OIG. (2019). Management alert: DHS needs to address dangerous overcrowding and prolonged detention of children and adults in the Rio Grande Valley. Office of Inspector General, Department of Homeland Security.

Ortega, B. (2018). Border patrol failed to count hundreds of migrant deaths on US soil. *CNN*, www.cnn.com/2018/05/14/us/border-patrol-migrant-death-count-invs/index.html.

Page, B., & Shapiro, R. (1983). Effects of public opinion on policy. *American Political Science Review*, 77(1),175–190.

Parent, D., et al. (1994). *Conditions of Confinement: Juvenile detention and Corrections Facilities [Research Report]*. Washington, DC: US Department of Justice, Office of Juvenile Justice and Delinquency Prevention.

Paul, E. F. (2017). *Property Rights and Eminent Domain*, New York: Routledge.

Pérez, E. O. (2010). Explicit evidence on the import of implicit attitudes: The IAT and immigration policy judgments. *Political Behavior*, 32 (4),517–545.

Perez, E. O. (2015). Xenophobic rhetoric and Its political effects on immigrants and their Co-Ethnics. *American Journal of Political Science*, 59 (3),549–564.

Peters, R., Moskwik, M., & Miller, J. R. B. (2018). Nature divided, scientists united: US–Mexico border wall threatens biodiversity and binational conservation, *BioScience*, 68(2),740–743.

Pew Research Center. (2019). Unauthorized immigrant population trends for states, birth countries and regions. 12 June, www.pewhispanic.org/interactives/unauthorized-trends/.

Phillips, S., Hagan, J. M., & Rodriguez, N. (2006). Brutal borders? Examining the treatment of deportees during arrest and detention. *Social Forces*, 85 (1),93–109.

Quinnipac University. (2018). Stop taking the kids, 66 percent of US voters say, Quinnipac University national poll finds: Support for Dreamers is 79 percent. Press release, 18 June, https://poll.qu.edu/national/release-detail?ReleaseID=2550.

Raaijmakers, E. A. C., et al. (2017). Exploring the relationship between subjectively experienced severity of imprisonment and recidivism: A neglected element in testing deterrence theory. *Journal of Research in Crime and Delinquency*, 54(1),3–28.

Radtke, D. (2017). Study: Fox News covered immigration five times as much as CNN and MSNBC combined. *Media Matters*, www.mediamatters.org/breitbart-news/study.

Radwan, C. (2019). AMA calls out the conditions of detention facilities. *Contemporary Pediatrics*, www.contemporarypediatrics.com/pediatrics/ama-calls.

Ramirez, M. D., & Petersen, D. A. M. (2020). *Ignored Racism: White Animus Towards Latinos*, New York: Cambridge University Press.

Rajaram, P. K. (2003). The spectacle of detention: Theatre, poetry and imagery in the contest over identity, security and responsibility in contemporary Australia. Asia Research Institute Working Paper Series No. 7.

Redden, M. (2014). Why are immigration detention facilities so cold? *Mother Jones*, www.motherjones.com/politics/2014/07/why-are. July 16.

Redlawsk, D. P. (2002). Hot cognition or cool consideration? Testing the effects of motivated reasoning on political decision making. *The Journal of Politics*, 64(4),1021–1044.

Reny, T., & Manzano, S. (2016). The negative effects of mass media stereotypes of Latinos and immigrants. In G. Ruhrmann, Y. Shooman, & P. Widmann, eds., *Media and Minorities: Questions on Representation from an International Perspective*, 195–212.

Reyes, J. R. (2018). Immigration detention: Recent trends and scholarship, Center for Migration Studies. 26 Mar., https://cmsny.org/publications/virtual brief-detention/.

Riva, S. (2017). Across the border and into the cold: Hieleras and the punishment of asylum-seeking Central American women in the United States. *Citizenship studies*, 21(3),309–326.

Rodrigo, C. M. (2018). AP: Migrant children may be adopted after parents are deported. *The Hill*, October 9, https://thehill.com/policy/international/amer icas/410653-ap-migrant-children-may-be-adopted-after-parents-are-deported.

Roediger, D. (2018). *Working toward Whiteness: How America's Immigrants Became White: The Strange Journal from Ellis Island to the Suburbs*, New York: Basic Books.

Rosenblum, M. (2012). *Border Security: Immigration Enforcement Between Ports of Entry*, Congressional Research Service.

Rouse, S .M. (2013) *Latinos in the Legislative Process: Interests and Influence*, New York: Cambridge University Press.

Ryo, E. (2018). Detention as deterrence. *Stan. L. Rev. Online*, 71, 237.

Ryo, E. (2019). Understanding immigration detention: Causes, conditions, and consequences, *Annual Review of Law and Social Science*, 15, 97–115.

Ryo, E., & Peacock, I. (2018). A national study of immigration detention in the United States. Center for Law and Social Science Research Paper Series No. CLASS18-19.

Sachetti, M. (2019) "Kids in cages": House hearing examines immigration detention as democrats push for more information. *The Washington Post*, July 10, www.washingtonpost.com/immigration/kids-in-cages-house-hearing-to-examine-immigration-detention-as-democrats-push-for-more-information /2019/07/10/3cc53006-a28f-11e9-b732-41a79c2551bf_story.html.

Sanchez, G. R., et al. (2015). Stuck between a rock and a hard place: The relationship between Latino/a's personal connections to immigrants and issue salience and presidential approval. *Politics Groups and Identities*, 3(3),454–468.

Santa Ana, O. (2002). *Brown Tide Rising: Metaphors of Latinos in Contemporary American Public Discourse*, Austin: University of Texas Press.

Sassen, S. (1988). *The Mobility of Labor and Capital: A Study in International Investment and Labor Flow*, New York: Cambridge University Press.

Sassen, S. (2014). *Expulsion: Brutality and Complexity in the Global Economy*, Cambridge: Harvard University Press.

Sawyer, A. (2019). Another needless death in US immigration detention. *Human Rights Watch*, www.hrw.org/news/2019/07/26/another-needless-death-us-immigration-detention.

Schaffner, B., MacWilliams, M., & Nteta, T. (2018). Understanding white polarization in the 2016 vote for president: The sobering role of racism and sexism. *Political Science Quarterly*, 133(1), DOI:10.1002/polq.12737.

Shear, M., and Hirschfeld Davis, J. (2019). Shoot migrants' legs, build alligator moat: Behind Trump's ideas for border. *New York Times*, October 2, www.nytimes.com/2019/10/01/us/politics/trump-border-wars.html.

Schildkraut, D. J. (2005). *Press One for English: Language Policy, Public Opinion, and American Identity*. Princeton: Princeton University Press

Schrag, P. (2020). *Baby Jails: The Fight to End the Incarceration of Refugee Children in America*. Oakland: University of California Press.

Schriro, D. (2010). Improving conditions of confinement for criminal inmates and immigrant detainees. *Am. Crim. L. Rev.*, 47, 1441.

Schriro, D. (2017a). Women and children first: An inside look at the challenges to reforming family detention in the United States. In M. Flynn & M. Flynn, eds., *Challenging Immigrant Detention: Academics, Activists, and Policymakers*, Northampton, MA: Edward Elgar Publishing.

Schriro, D. (2017b). Weeping in the playtime of others: The Obama administration's failed reform of ICE family detention practices. *Journal on Migration and Human Security*, 5(2),452–480.

Sharma, N. (2007). Global apartheid and nation-statehood: Instituting border regimes. In J. Goodman and P. James, eds., *Nationalism and Global Solidarities: Alternative Projections to Neoliberal Globalisation*, New York: Routledge.

Sherman, C., Mendoza, M. & Burke, G. (2019). US held record number of migrant children in custody in 2019. *Associated Press*, https://apnews.com/015702afdb4d4fbf85cf5070cd2c6824.

Sides, J., Tesler, M., & Vavreck, L. (2017). The 2016 U.S. election: How Trump lost and won. *Journal of Democracy*, 28(2),34–44.

Sierra Club. (2015). *Border Wall Environmental Impacts*, Sierra Club.

Silva, D. (2018). 'Like I am trash': Migrant children reveal stories of detention, separation. *NBC News*, www.nbcnews.com/news/latino/i-am-trash-migrant-children-reveal-stories-detention-separation-n895006.

Silva, D. (2019). Judge blocks Trump administration from indefinitely detaining migrant children. *NBC News*, www.nbcnews.com/news/latino/judge-blocks-trump-administration-indefinitely-detaining-migrant-children-n1059816.

Silverman, S. (2010). Immigration detention in America: A history of its expansion and a study of its significance. Center on Migration, Policy and Society, Working paper No. 80.

Simon, J. (1998). Refugees in a carceral age: The rebirth of immigration prisons in the United States. *Public Culture*, 10(3),577–607.

Skocpol, T., & Williamson, V. (2016). *The Tea Party and the Remaking of Republican Conservatism*, New York: Oxford University Press

Slack, J., Martinez, D., Whiteford, S., & Peiffer, E. (2015). In harm's way: Family separation, immigration enforcement programs and security on the US–Mexico border. *Journal on Migration and Human Security*, 3(20),109–128.

Smith, D., & Phillips, T. (2018). Child separations: Trump faces extreme backlash from public and his own party. *The Guardian*, www.theguardian.com/us-news/2018/jun/19/child.

Smith, S. (2019). Christians speak out as migrant children are detained without soap, hygiene needs. *Christian Post*, www.christianpost.com/news/christians-speak-out-as-migrant-children-are-detained-without-soap-hygiene-needs.html.

Sonmez, F., & Parker, A. (2020). As Trump stands by Charlottesville remarks, rise of white-nationalist violence becomes an issue in 2020 presidential race. *Washington Post*, www.washingtonpost.com/politics/as-trump-stands-by-charlottesville-remarks-rise-of-white-nationalist-violence-becomes-an-issue-in-2020-presidential-race/2019/04/28/83aaf1ca-69c0-11e9-a66d-a82d3f3d96d5_story.html%3foutputtype=amp.

Sorel, J. (2014). Is the Wall Soluble into International Law? In E. Vallet, ed., *Borders, Fences and Walls*, New York: Routledge.

Stieb, M. (2019). Everything we know about the inhumane conditions at migrant detention camps. *New York Magazine*, http://nymag.com/intelligencer/2019/06/the-inhumane-conditions-at-migrant-detention-camps.html.

Stiglitz, J. (2018). *Globalization and Its Discontents: Anti-globalization in the Era of Trump*, New York: W.W. Norton & Company.

Stolberg, S. G. (2019). Ocasio-Cortez calls migrant detention centers "concentration camps," backlash. *The New York Times*, www.nytimes.com/2019/06/18/us/politics/ocasio-cortez.

Suárez-Orozco, C., Bang, H. J., & Kim, H. Y. (2011). I felt like my heart was staying behind: Psychological implications of family separations & reunifications for immigrant youth. *Journal of Adolescent Research*, 26 (2),222–257.

Taber, C. S., & Lodge, M. (2006). Motivated skepticism in the evaluation of political beliefs. *American Journal of Political Science*, 50(3),755–769.

Takei, G. (2018). "At least during the internment . . . : Are words I never thought I'd utter. *Foreign Policy*, https://foreignpolicy.com/2018/06/19/at-least-during-the-internment-are-words-i-thought-id-never-utter-family-separation-children-border/.

Taylor, J. (2019). State of the Union: "Tonight, I ask you to choose greatness," Trump says. *NPR*, www.npr.org/2019/02/05/688043654/watch-live.

Tesler, M. (2016). *Post-Racial or Most-Racial?: Race and Politics in the Obama Era*, Chicago: University of Chicago Press.

Thompson, A. C. (2019). Inside the secret border patrol Facebook group where agents joke about migrant deaths and post sexist memes. *ProPublica*, www.propublica.org/article/secret-border-patrol-facebook-group-agents-joke-about-migrant-deaths-post-sexist-memes.

Tichenor, D. (2002). *Dividing Lines: The Politics of Immigration Control in America*, Princeton: Princeton University Press.

Trapasso, C. (2019). The real border wall battle: It's Texas homeowners who may pay the price. *MySA*, www.mysanantonio.com/realestate/article/Thousands-of-People-Will-Lose-Their-13612620.php.

Trump, D. J. (2016). Transcript of Donald Trump's immigration speech. *The New York Times*, www.nytimes.com/2016/09/02/us/politics/transcript-trump.

Trump, D. J. (2019a). President Donald J. Trump's efforts to combat the crisis at our southern border are delivering results. *The White House*, www.whitehouse.gov/briefings-statements/president.

Trump, D. J. (2019b). President Donald Trump stands by his declaration of a national emergency on the southern border. March 15. *The White House*, www.whitehouse.gov/briefings-statements/president-donald-j-trump-stands-declaration-national-emergency-southern-border/.

Tuch, S. A. & Hughes, M. (2011). Whites' racial policy attitudes in the Twenty-first century: The continuing significance of racial resentment. *The ANNALS of the American Academy of Political and Social Science*, 634(1),134–152.

U.S. Border Patrol. (2019). Southwest Border Sectors: Southwest Border Deaths by Fiscal Year. www.cbp.gov/document/stats/us-border-patrol-fiscal-year-southwest-border-sector-deaths-fy-1998-fy-2019.

Valdez, I. (2016). Punishment, race, and the organization of US immigration exclusion. *Political Research Quarterly*, 69(4),640–654.

Valentino, N. A., & Brader, T. (2011) The sword's other edge: Perceptions of discrimination and racial policy opinion after Obama. *Public Opinion Quarterly*, 75(2),201–226.

Valentino, N. A., Brader, T., & Jardina, A. E. (2013). Immigration opposition among US whites: General ethnocentrism or media priming of attitudes about Latinos. *Political Psychology*, 34(2),149–166.

Vallet, E. (2016) *Borders, Fences and Walls*, New York: Routledge

Vallet, E. (2019). Border walls and the illusion of deterrence. In J. Reece, ed., *Open Borders: In Defense of Free Movement*, Borgart: University of Georgia Press.

Vallet, E., & David, C. (2014). Walls of Money: Secrutization of Border Discourses and Militarization of Markets. In E. Vallet, ed., *Borders, Fences and Walls*, New York: Routledge.

Vallet, E., & David, C. -P. (2012). Introduction: The (Re)Building of the wall in international relations. *Journal of Borderlands Studies*, 27(2),111–119.

Wadhia, S. S. (2019). *Banned: Immigration Enforcement in the Time of Trump*, New York: New York University Press.

Wallace, G. P. R., & Wallace, S. J. (2020). Who gets to have a DREAM? Examining public support for immigration reform. *International Migration Review*, 54(2),527–558.

Wallace, S. J. (2012). It's complicated: Latinos, President Obama, and the 2012 election. *Social Science Quarterly*, 93(5),1360–1383.

Wallace, S. J. (2014a). Papers please: State-level anti-immigrant legislation in the wake of Arizona's SB 1070. *Political Science Quarterly*, 129(2),261–291.

Wallace, S. J. (2014b). Representing Latinos: Examining descriptive and substantive representation in Congress. *Political Research Quarterly*, 67 (4),917–929.

Washington Post. (2018). Mother reunited with son: They told me they would put him up for adoption. *Washington Post*, www.washingtonpost.com/video/national/segments/mother-reunited-with-son-they-told-me-they-would-put-him-up-for-adoption/2018/06/22/bbeb9b8e-7646-11e8-bda1-18e53a448a14_video.html.

Weber, L., & Pickering, S. (2011). *Globalization and Borders: Death at the Global Frontier*, New York, NY: Palgrave.

Welch, M. (1996). The immigration crisis: Detention as an emerging mechanism of social control, *Social Justice*,23(3), 169–184.

Willis, A. (2019a). U.S. House passes $4.5 billion border aid bill amid mounting concern for detained migrant children. *The Texas Tribune*, www.texastribune.org /2019/06/25/us-house.

Willis, A. (2019b). Here's what's in the $4.6 billion border aid bill passed by Congress. *The Texas Tribune*, www.texastribune.org/2019/06/27/border-aid.

Wilper, A. P., et al. (2009). The health and health care of US prisoners: Results of a nationwide survey. *American Journal of Public Health*, 99 (4),666–672.

Wilsher, D. (2011). *Immigration Detention: Law, History, Politics*. New York: Cambridge University Press.

Wilson, J. G., Benavides, J., Reisinger, A., Lemen, J., Hurwitz, Z., Spangler, J., & Engle, K. (2008). An analysis of demographic disparities associated with the proposed U.S.–Mexico border fence in Cameron County, Texas. University of Texas School of Law Working Group on Human Rights and the Border Wall.

Wong, C. J. (2010). *Boundaries of Obligation in American Politics: Geographic, National, and Racial Communities*. New York: Cambridge University Press.

Wong, T. K. (2015). *Rights, Deportation, and Detention in the Age of Immigration*, Stanford: Stanford University Press.

Wong, T. K. (2017). *The Politics of Immigration: Partisanship, Demographic Change, and American National Identity*, New York: Oxford University Press.

Wong, T. K. (2018). Do family separation and detention deter immigration? https://perma.cc/EXR5-7VGL.

Wong, T .K., & Ramakrishnan, S. K. (2010). Partisanship not Spanish: Explaining municipal ordinances affecting undocumented immigrants. In M. Varsanyi, ed., *Taking Local Control: Immigration Policy Activism in US Cities and States*, Palo Alto: Stanford University Press.

Wu, N. (2019). Trump administration to house migrant children at Fort Sill, which once served as a Japanese internment camp. *USA Today*, www .usatoday.com/story/news/politics/2019/06/12/trump-administration-house-migrant-kids-former-japanese-internment-camp/1430394001/.

Zepeda-Millán, C. (2014). Perceptions of threat, demographic diversity, and the framing of illegality: Explaining (non)participation in New York's 2006 immigrant protests. *Political Research Quarterly*, 67(4),880–888.

Zepeda-Millán, C. (2017). *Latino Mass Mobilization: Immigration, Racialization, and Activism*, New York: Cambridge University Press.

Zimmer, B. (2019). What Trump talks about when he talks about infestations. *Politico*, www.politico.com/magazine/story/2019/07/29/trump-baltimore-infest-tweet-cummings-racist-227485.

Zolberg, A. (2006). *A Nation by Design: Immigration Policy in the Fashioning of America*, Cambridge: Harvard University Press.

Acknowledgments

Attempting to write a book about President Trump's border wall, family separation, and child detention practices as these historic events unfolded was both difficult and depressing. Ultimately, we accepted that there was no way we could ever capture the full dynamics of these "moving targets" given our deadline and word limitation. Thus, while we take full responsibility for the shortcomings of this manuscript, we would like to thank our editors at Cambridge, Megan Ming Francis and Sara Doskow, for their patience and faith in the importance of this project. Our copy editor, Ruth Homrighaus, undoubtedly improved the prose and was vital in making every word count. We would also like to thank the reviewers for their feedback, as well as our research assistants – Olivia Marti, Julia Wejchert, and Dennis Young – for their help. Parts of this Element were presented at the UC–Berkeley Race, Ethnicity, and Immigration Colloquium, and we are grateful for the excellent comments we received from participants, especially Cybelle Fox, Desmond Jagmohan, Cristina Mora, and Eric Schickler. Other segments of the book were inspired or significantly informed by discussions with activist friends in Berlin, Los Angeles, and Tijuana, especially Elias Steinhilper, Jana Ciernioch, Xiomara Corpeño, Jessica Viramontes, David Vasquez, Saul Sarabia, Aura Bogado, and Nicole Ramos. We are truly appreciative of the many colleagues who offered us critical advice, suggestions, and resources, including Phil Ayoub, JR DeShazo, Dan Gillion, Michael Jones-Correa, Chris Parker, Efrén Pérez, Rene Rocha, Emily Ryo, Al Tillery, and Shatema Threadcraft. We owe a tremendous amount of gratitude to Geoff Wallace and Stephanie Castro for reading multiple drafts of the manuscript and offering us generous comments. Sophia would also like to thank her children for their patience while mom finished her book with *tío* Chris and her sister and parents for always being just a phone call away.

We would like to dedicate this book to Geoff and Stephanie for their unwavering support and partnership, and to migrants around the world who dare to cross deadly borders in hopes of better lives for themselves and their families.

Cambridge Elements ≡

Race, Ethnicity, and Politics

Megan Ming Francis
University of Washington

Megan Ming Francis is an Associate Professor of Political Science at the University of Washington and a Fellow at the Ash Center for Democratic Governance and the Carr Center for Human Rights at the Harvard Kennedy School. Francis is the author of the award winning book, *Civil Rights and the Making of the Modern American State*. She is particularly interested in American political and constitutional development, social movements, the criminal punishment system, Black politics, philanthropy, and the post-Civil War South.

About the Series

Elements in Race, Ethnicity, and Politics is an innovative publishing initiative in the social sciences. The series publishes important original research that breaks new ground in the study of race, ethnicity, and politics. It welcomes research that speaks to the current political moment, research that provides new perspectives on established debates, and interdisciplinary research that sheds new light on previously understudied topics and groups.

Cambridge Elements $\equiv$

Race, Ethnicity, and Politics

Elements in the Series

A full series listing is available at www.cambridge.org/EREP

Made in the USA
Las Vegas, NV
07 September 2021

29775373R00065